"Phil's heart for discipleship is evident from the start. Challenging a 'fast food' approach to the Christian life, he outlines a methodology for becoming a committed disciple of Christ. This book provides a much-needed approach for strengthening God's church for both mission and service, showing us what it takes to live as true representatives of God."

—Rev. John Delancey, director of Biblical Israel Ministries & Tours and author of *Devotional Treasures from the Holy Land*

"*D²* is one of the few books on discipleship I have seen that offers a clear path to knowing God in a more intimate way. Phil answers the practical questions of 'Why?' 'What?' and 'How?' in a manner accessible for everyone. I highly recommend this book to anyone who has a longing to dive deeper in their faith."

—Jackie Halstead, founder and CEO of the Selah Center for Spiritual Formation

"With the simple image of fast-food Christianity, Phil asks us to think about what we are truly converted *to*. We are all inevitably discipling someone to something, but what if what we are leading them to makes little difference? There is, as this book makes clear, a 'more excellent way.'"

—Randy Harris, instructor, Department of Bible, Missions, and Ministry, Abilene Christian University, and author of *Living Jesus*

"When relegated to theory, spiritual formation becomes only an abstraction. McKinney's volume refreshingly repudiates this notion by providing readers with rock-solid spiritual practices for the heart, soul, and mind. Both individuals and small groups will benefit from his explanation of discipleship, one that is accessible to all maturing disciples of Jesus."

—David Wray, professor emeritus of Bible, Abilene Christian University

"This is a thorough and honest explanation of the challenges and great blessings of discipleship. McKinney dissects the cultural forces preventing us from following Jesus and offers a plan for getting in step with the Spirit. It's a reminder of the simple, but high, hopes Jesus has for our discipleship. The church needs this book!"

—Houston Heflin, associate professor of ministry, Abilene Christian University, author of *Pray Like You Breathe*

"Ministers and Bible teachers speak a lot about being a disciple and call their listeners to various actions, but it often feels like a consumeristic, shallow attempt to increase membership and involvement. If we truly want to be followers of Christ, we must define discipleship and identify the real benefits of participating in the difficult journey of becoming a mature follower of Christ.

This is why I love D^2. It introduces us to a practical, well thought-out journey from nominal acceptance to maturity in Christ. I will be using this book to strengthen my teaching as well as my own personal journey of discipleship."

—David Fraze, director of youth ministry, Lubbock Christian University, and author of *Practical Wisdom for Youth Ministry*

"If we take it seriously, Jesus's provocative command to 'make disciples' will transform the Christian life and his church. Phil's message rightly shifts our focus from a program-driven perspective of discipleship to one that is relational, involving the whole person and the whole church. Employing a wide range of resources, Phil offers a vibrant, biblical view of discipleship with plenty of on-the-ground application."

—Phil Howard, professor of ministry leadership and spiritual formation, Toccoa Falls College

"Grounded in biblical narrative and personal experience, Phil's insights are partnered with constructive and practical ways for Christians to develop a deeper, more authentic relationship with God. I highly recommend this book to Christians who want to engage more purposefully in their walk of faith."

—Ben Pickett, discipleship minister at the Highland Church of Christ, Abilene, TX

"Thousands of books have been written on discipleship. Yet Phil writes with a fresh voice, sharing how discipleship works best when it is understood and practiced in community. Every eldership, ministry staff, and leadership team needs to dive into D^2 and gain a better understanding of how to live out and teach discipleship in their immediate context."

—Josh Ross, lead minister at Sycamore View Church in Memphis, TN, and author of *Scarred Faith* and *Re\entry*

"If you are serious about Christian spiritual formation being more than theory, roll up your sleeves and take the intentional message and guidance of $D2$ into your life. In this book, Phil demonstrates his passion for discipleship and his compassion for those who want to be transformed but have been trapped by ineffective methods. Not simply a how-to book, D^2 will challenge you to become the person you are called to be."

—Daniel Stockstill, associate dean, College of Bible and Ministry, Harding University

"Phil McKinney offers readers the fruit of a congregation's study and reflection on discipleship. Suitable for small groups and Bible classes, D^2 outlines a curriculum for becoming disciples and disciple-makers. This timely book reflects the experience of McKinney's long tenure with a vibrant church."

—Carson Reed, vice president for church relations and executive director of the Siburt Institute for Church Ministry, Abilene Christian University

D²

BECOMING A DEVOTED

FOLLOWER OF CHRIST

PHIL McKINNEY II

LEAFWOOD
PUBLISHERS
an imprint of Abilene Christian University Press

D²
Becoming a Devoted Follower of Christ

LEAFWOOD
P U B L I S H E R S
an imprint of Abilene Christian University Press

Copyright © 2019 by Phil McKinney II

ISBN 978-1-68426-180-2

Printed in the United States of America

LIBRARY OF CONGRESS CATALOGING-IN-PUBLICATION DATA
Names: McKinney, Phil, II, 1973- author.
Title: D2 : becoming a devoted follower of Christ / Phil McKinney II, Ph.D.
Other titles: D2 : becoming a devoted follower of Christ | D squared :
    becoming a devoted follower of Christ | Becoming a devoted follower of Christ
Description: Abilene, Texas : Leafwood Publishers, [2019]
Identifiers: LCCN 2018035670 | ISBN 9781684261802 (pbk.)
Subjects: LCSH: Spiritual formation. | Discipling (Christianity)
Classification: LCC BV4511 .M4525 2019 | DDC 248.4—dc23
LC record available at https://lccn.loc.gov/ 2018035670

Cover design by ThinkPen Design
Interior text design by Strong Design, Sandy Armstrong

Leafwood Publishers is an imprint of Abilene Christian University Press
ACU Box 29138
Abilene, Texas 79699

1-877-816-4455
www.leafwoodpublishers.com

19 20 21 22 23 24 / 7 6 5 4 3 2 1

Contents

Preface

The book you hold in your hands is the product of a long journey that began in the fall of 2008. As I began my ministry at Fairfax Church of Christ, I was asked to add on to my role the oversight of spiritual formation and discipleship. I was blessed to begin this journey with a team of people who desperately wanted to see our church family grow more in their faith and in their relationship with God. Many discussions on this topic had already been held before my arrival, but when we all came together, God began to share with our team a vision for spiritual formation and discipleship at Fairfax. We didn't know how it would look specifically, but we knew we had to be faithful to that vision.

So we spent six months praying, fasting, studying, and seeking the guidance of the Holy Spirit. After that time of discovery, we felt that God had laid out for us a plan for spiritual formation and discipleship. We began to share that plan with our leadership, our ministry leaders, and finally the entire congregation in the spring and fall of 2009. A great deal of excitement simmered as we shared with everyone how we wanted to be intentional with our spiritual growth. We began to implement several aspects of the plan, yet we knew that these aspects were only the first steps and that God would continue to shape the plan and show us what he wanted for his people at Fairfax.

This book is the result of that journey. So although the book you now hold was originally intended to help all of our family members define and understand our plan for discipleship at Fairfax, it is now an opportunity to help you in your desire to grow more and more like Jesus every day. The goal of this book is to assist you in becoming a devoted follower of Jesus Christ who passionately leads others to him.

I hope this book will help you answer the questions of Why? (Chapter One), What? (Chapters Two, Three, and Four), and How? (Chapters Five and Six). Chapter Seven and the appendix are designed to help you move toward becoming a disciple who makes disciples. I am excited to offer this book to you with the hope that it will help you move toward a deeper relationship with Christ in which his Holy Spirit forms, conforms, and transforms you into the image of our Lord and Savior, Jesus Christ.

As with any work like this, many people made it possible. I would like to first thank God for revealing all of this to us. For me, this journey began at a retreat center where I spent the day in prayer and fasting and God began to open up the Scriptures to me in a way that I had never seen before. He continues to do that today, so I cannot help but thank him and give him all the glory and honor for this work.

I must also recognize two particular groups at Fairfax Church of Christ. First, I need to recognize and honor our elders. Through the years, they have done nothing but support and encourage me toward this work. They have prayed for me, with me, and over me. I love each of you deeply and am thankful for your presence and encouragement in my life. The second group is our Discipleship Team at Fairfax Church of Christ (both past and present). When we began this journey, it was with a team made up of Bruce Black, Lisa Bosley, Andrea Morris, Dave Palmer, Dwayne Phillips, Darla Robinson, Ellyn Sergio, Dakota Wood, and Sammie and Jill Young. Without these individuals, this book could not have come about.

As the years have gone on, several other individuals have served on our Discipleship Team and have contributed to this book in thought and spirit, including Todd Batt, Ray Bingham, Dennis Cesone, Erin Gulick, Deb Holder, Sam Jeffrey, P. J. McGuire, Mike Miller, Logan Morris, Chad Mynatt, Alecia Nault, Benn and Laura Oltmann, Andy Pierce, Rebecca Poole, Paul Reiman, Ken Smith, Rita Strydom, Kyle Symanowitz, Tyler Travis, Carie Whittaker, and Lori Windham. Thank you all so much for your words of wisdom and guidance through this journey together. I would also like to express a very special thank you to Ashley Young for being my resident editor. You saved me tons of work and made this book so much better! Thank you!

I would be remiss if I did not also thank my family and, in particular, my wife, Angie. Through the years, Angie has been patient with me when I was away for conferences, school, meetings, and so much more, all for the sake of developing this book and fostering discipleship. Both she and my daughters (Kaylee, Taylor, and Rylie) have sacrificed time with me so that this could come to fruition. Thank you all so much! Words could never express my love and appreciation to these beautiful ladies in my life. I thank my God every time I think of you.

May this work bring glory to God and expand his kingdom here on this earth and on through eternity. Now, let's go!

Phil McKinney II

Follow Me

My relationship with Jesus has reached a new level of intensity, and I want to tell you about it.

I can't remember when I didn't love Jesus. Yes, like everyone else, I struggled with and questioned my faith in Jesus, but deep down, I have always been awed by his perfection and his power. But, like most of his followers, it was only as I matured spiritually that I became aware of how much I was missing. Eventually, it was some of our Lord's most familiar words—the greatest commands in Mark 12 and the Great Commission at the end of Matthew 28— that opened new windows for me to see Christian discipleship in an array of colors I had not perceived before. As I plunged into a more serious study of this subject, I began to speak of the new disciple dynamics I was discovering as D^2—a shorthand way to refer to becoming a devoted follower of Christ. This study changed my life. Let me share it with you in the pages that follow.

Today, we hear a great deal of discussion about discipleship and spiritual formation and many differing opinions about what it is and how to define it. I have spent a great deal of time in prayer, fasting, and study to seek the Lord and what he says concerning his call to make disciples and how that impacts his body of believers. Perhaps I should explain right here that I align myself with no special group of individuals who have made claims concerning discipleship and spiritual formation. Instead, I recognize the inevitability of discipleship and spiritual formation for those who have declared their dependence on Jesus and who truly desire to love and seek him daily. So I decided to be intentional about my efforts to foster spiritual growth that leads one toward transformation into the image of Christ.

My mission is God's mission. It is my desire to do all I can (through God's power and the leading of his Spirit) to ensure that the family of God seeks to make devoted followers of Jesus Christ who passionately lead others to him, both on an individual level and as a collective whole. In fact, this is the mission for all God's people. C. S. Lewis put it this way:

> Every Christian is to become a *little Christ*. The whole purpose of becoming a Christian is simply nothing else. . . . In the same way the Church exists for nothing else but to draw men into Christ, to make them *little Christs*. If they are not doing that, all the cathedrals, clergy, missions, sermons, even the Bible itself, are simply a waste of time. God became Man for no other purpose.[1]

So, on an individual level, my goal is to become a disciple who makes disciples. On a larger scale, as a church family, we want to make disciples who make disciples—to do and be what I call D².

But before we can start making disciples, each of us must make a personal decision to become a true follower of Christ.

"Follow Me"

Two words that changed the course of twelve unlikely individuals in the first century. Two words that should also change the course of our lives today. But do they? Do we follow Jesus in the way the early disciples chose to follow him? Do we drop everything without reservation to follow him as our Lord and Savior? Or do we follow him in name alone? Are we satisfied with wearing the name "Christian" without being transformed by the Holy Spirit into his image? Are we satisfied with being "Christians" who receive the salvation that Jesus gives without becoming the people Jesus calls us to be?

For too long, churches have based their success on numbers. Success has been measured by how many members the church has, how nice and big their building is, how many people they baptize in a year, or even how big their budget is.[2] However, the true measure of success in any church is not their size. Measured success in the Lord's church is evidenced by his people being formed, conformed, and transformed into his image. Are we truly becoming more like Christ?

While evidence of this sort of transformation may be difficult to quantify, it is demonstrated in the spiritual fruit that disciples bear in their homes, churches, and communities at large. The real question that must be answered is this: What are we moving people toward? Are we simply interested in gaining members and satisfied with developing people into converts rather than disciples, or are we helping every person walk down the path of becoming a true disciple of Christ?

A "convert" is a person who has been persuaded to change his or her religious faith or other beliefs. However, one can easily be

15

a convert without being a disciple who follows Christ with total abandonment. The church has for too long focused on making converts rather than making disciples. As Dallas Willard notes, "The making of *converts*, or church members, has become the mandatory goal of Christian ministers—if even that—while the making of disciples is pushed to the very margins of Christian existence. Many Christian groups simply have no idea what discipleship is and have relegated it to para-church organizations." He goes on to say that the elephant in the church today is "non-discipleship": "The fundamental negative reality among Christian believers now is their failure to be constantly learning how to live their lives in The Kingdom Among Us. And it is an *accepted* reality."[3] We have enabled a division among professing Christians: those who are truly and wholly devoted to Christ and those who maintain a consumer, client-based relationship with Christ and his church.

A professor and mentor of mine, Dr. Dan Stockstill, once said to me, "What we win them with is what we win them to." During all my years of ministry, this phrase has stuck with me. For my first ten-plus years of ministry, I chose to win people to a consumeristic mindset of Christ and his church. I was more concerned about acceptance and being liked than with truly helping people become the disciples Jesus called them to be. I won them to a "fast-food" Christianity and led them to become members of the "Club of Christ." Let me explain.

Fast-Food Christianity

In our consumeristic "me-centered" culture, we are often led to live our lives with a fast-food mentality. We all know what fast-food restaurants offer us—a quick source of less-than-quality food, right when we want it. But why do we choose fast food? Here are some reasons:

- **Replacement of responsibility.** Fast food replaces our responsibility to prepare and cook our meal. Instead, when we don't feel like cooking, we jump into the car and head to the nearest fast-food restaurant. We don't have to work; someone else can do it for us.
- **Cheap.** Fast food is not going to cost us a lot unless we want extra and are willing to pay for it. Yet even with the extras added on, fast food is typically not costly.
- **Choices.** With fast food, we can choose from several different options to suit our immediate needs and desires. The choice is ours, from choosing the restaurant to choosing the menu items.
- **Service with no strings attached.** With fast food, not only do we get what we want, we are also served by others with little to no contact. We are not required to form any lasting relationships. We order our food, are served, and move on. If we don't like the service, we complain to the manager. If we don't like the food, we take it back and ask that it be replaced according to our liking. We are not required to offer gratuity.
- **Quick.** Fast food typically lives up to its name. We want it now; we get it now. We make our request and expect it promptly.
- **Drive-through service.** With fast food, if we don't want to go in and sit down, we have the option of simply staying in our car, ordering through a microphone, making our payment, picking up our food, and driving off.

What does all this have to do with our approach to being a Christian? Consider how our approach to Christ is like our approach to fast food: No investment. No attachments. Just fast delivery with superficial interaction as we want it. Is this our approach to Christ? What might a fast-food approach to Christianity look like?

- **Replacement of responsibility.** Fast-food Christianity replaces our responsibility to grow in our relationship with Christ and live our life for him. Instead, when we don't feel like doing it ourselves, we jump into the car and head to the nearest church and expect someone else to feed us spiritually. We don't have to work; someone else can do it for us—someone who's paid to do it.

- **Cheap.** Fast-food Christianity is not going to cost us a lot unless we want extra and are willing to pay for it. Yet even with the extras added on, fast-food Christianity typically is not costly and will only require us to serve, to reach out, and to give occasionally (if at all). The amount we serve, reach out, and give is up to us and based on how much time and money we are willing to invest in the moment.

- **Choices.** With fast-food Christianity, we can choose from several different options to suit our immediate needs and desires. The choice is ours—from choosing the church to choosing what and how much we will be involved.

- **Service with no strings attached.** With fast-food Christianity, not only do we get what we want, but we are also served by others with little to no contact. We are not required to form any lasting relationships. We order off the spiritual menu, are served by those paid to serve (and those crazy volunteer types), and move on. If we don't like the service, we complain to the church leaders and staff members without volunteering to work to make it better. If we don't like the spiritual food, we take it back and ask that it be replaced according to our liking. If our order still doesn't meet our satisfaction, we move on to another choice.

- **Quick.** Fast-food Christianity typically lives up to its name. We want it now; we get it now. We make our request to the elders and staff members about how and what we would like changed, and we expect it promptly. We want a quick sermon that meets our immediate needs so we can leave quickly. If it isn't quick and it doesn't get to the point that we want to hear, then we stand up and walk out without paying.
- **Drive-through service.** With fast-food Christianity, if we don't want to be too involved, we have the option of simply coming in for worship (coming late is an option because we must be at work and school on time all week long, so we need a break from being on time), ordering our worship and spiritual food, making our payment (though only if there's money left or the church is spending the money the way we think it should), picking up our worship and spiritual food, and driving off. Maybe we'll go to Bible class, but that is optional, and we don't expect anything else.

No investment. No attachments. Is this how Jesus envisioned his disciples? Is a drive-through relationship all that the Lord requires of us? Or is there more to this whole "follow me" bit? The Bible makes it very clear what the Lord requires. It shows us what being a disciple of Christ might look like:

- **Responsibility.** Christianity (being a disciple of Christ) requires us to be responsible for our own spiritual growth and to live a life that honors God and reflects Christ. Because we have been crucified with Christ, we can't pawn off our responsibility on anyone else. Read Hebrews 5:11–6:3 and Galatians 2:20.
- **Costly.** Christianity (being a disciple of Christ) costs us everything. Our money, our possessions, our

time—everything is his. Our salvation cost Jesus everything. Do you think he requires anything less from us? His grace is free, but it wasn't cheap. "You were bought with a price" (1 Cor. 6:20; 7:23). Read Luke 14:25–33.

• **Only one choice.** Christianity (being a disciple of Christ) affords us only one choice: *Jesus.* That choice requires that everything we do be an honor and glory to him. It requires that we always be at our post as Christians. There is no option to be uninvolved. Discipleship requires involvement. Read John 14:6, 15, 21, 23–24 and 1 John 2:3–6.

• **Service with strings attached.** Christianity (being a disciple of Christ) requires us to serve rather than be served. That service requires us to work with others and to develop relationships as part of the body of Christ. We, therefore, build eternal relationships with our brothers and sisters, and it is *not* optional. Everyone is required to serve and build up the kingdom of God. This service cannot be delegated to paid staff members and church leadership. Complaining without helping to discover and implement a solution is not an option. And, by the way, the chosen solution may not be to our own personal liking. Read Mark 10:42–45; Philippians 2:1–18; and 1 John 3:16–19.

• **Slow and at times painful.** Christianity (being a disciple of Christ) does not happen fast and is a life-long and eternal process. The seeds we plant and the work we do may never produce fruit in our lifetime. As we labor, we will encounter suffering, pain, and change. Our desires may not be in God's plan and, therefore, will not happen. We must surrender our will to conform to his. Read 1 Corinthians 3:1–15; Philippians 1:3–6; Hebrews 11:32–40; and 1 Peter 1:6–12.

• **Commitment.** Christianity (being a disciple of Christ) requires total commitment. God will never be satisfied with just part of us. Involvement in Christ and his body is expected. Read Luke 9:23–26 and Hebrews 10:24–25.

This fast-food Christianity mindset has deeply impacted Christ's church. It has led us to approach the ministry of the church from a worldly view that contradicts God's intent for his people. Instead of helping people join God's family, the church, we have helped them become members of the Club of Christ. This concept deserves more explanation.

The Club of Christ

We all know what clubs are. They are associations or organizations that are dedicated to a particular interest or activity. Clubs offer individuals a way to join with other individuals for a common purpose. We often join clubs quickly and easily accept their membership requirements, no matter the costs or expectations. So why do we join clubs?

In considering the answer to this question, I searched what a local country club offered its members. The Country Club of Fairfax, Virginia, offers and requires many things.[4] What follows here is intended only for the sake of comparison, not as criticism.

I discovered that the club offers "family." By family, it means that it offers a wide array of activities that provide an opportunity for members to come together and build relationships. They also provide a place where special events can be held, such as weddings, special occasions, meetings, and seminars. It boasts that the club has experienced personnel who will be there to assist members with all their needs. It states that "no matter your interest, at the Country Club of Fairfax there is truly something for everyone."

As I read on, I discovered that it offers several types of memberships, from full membership with everything the club offers (including stock options) to tailored memberships to meet individual needs. What I found most interesting is that it offers a "social/house only" membership. One can simply come for the fellowship and community. If you think about it, people are willing to pay to have community. Each of the memberships has requirements and fees that accompany them.

So what does all that have to do with discipleship and the ministry of the church? Maybe nothing. Or maybe everything. I began to ask myself, "How is the church any different than a country club?" Consider how this view and approach of a secular country club might infiltrate how we approach the ministry of the church. What if we ran things like a Club of Christ? What would it look like? Perhaps our website would read:

> The Club of Christ is a private, member-owned club that provides exceptional family-oriented spiritual and social services and activities. As a friendly, family-oriented, and welcoming membership, the Club of Christ is a true reflection of the diversity of those living and working in the area and provides something for everyone.

> ### *Family*
> The Club of Christ provides families with exceptional spiritual and social opportunities. Whether it is our vibrant student ministry, our exceptional children's ministry and preschool, our exciting young adults ministry, or even our pulsating worship services, there is something for every family member to enjoy. In addition, our outstanding missions and outreach programs offer even more opportunities for our members to partake in, including optional mission opportunities and service projects, as well as personal training and Bible classes. With an ongoing and

active schedule, the Club is the perfect venue to bring
families together.

Special Events

We offer worship services, Bible classes, student
and children activities, and so much more
with a commitment to excellence that exceeds
your expectations.

Whether you are planning an age-appropriate activity or a small-group Bible study, your event will be
created especially for you.

Our experienced ministerial staff will work with
you to advise and assist you with the planning of your
function and selecting your personal spiritual menu.
Here at the Club, your spiritual growth will be exactly
the way you desire, as each worship event and activity
is individually planned and tailored with the most personal attention paid to the smallest detail.

The Club of Christ can accommodate large families,
and all arrangements can be discussed by contacting
our family life minister who will be delighted to discuss
your individual needs.

Activities

The Club of Christ provides members numerous
opportunities to become involved in our active and
enthusiastic community. The activities offered by
the Club cater to every age and ability and provide
members with the chance to learn, practice, or improve
their spiritual gifts.

The Club also offers activities that meet other interests as well, from various social outings to our women's
and men's ministries. Options abound outside of

traditional church offerings. No matter your interest, at the Club, there is truly something for everyone.

Membership Types
- Full membership
  Worship / Bible classes / small groups / service / missions / ministry activities (plus full stock in the church family)
- Half membership
  Worship / Bible classes / optional ministry activities (plus partial stock in the church family)
- Pew membership
  Worship / Optional Bible classes (no additional stock in the church family)

Age-Specific Memberships can be added at an additional fee. See below.
- Children's ministry (kids' worship / Bible classes / kid activities)—no parental involvement necessary
- Student ministry (teen Bible classes / missions / service / teen activities)—no parental involvement necessary
- Other ministry membership (based on personal needs and desires)

Contact the church office for membership fees and schedules. We are here to serve YOU!

Again, we must ask, is this what God envisioned for his people? Is this the bride Christ died for? Or is there more? Why will we quickly and easily join and meet the expectations of the Club of Christ, but only hesitantly involve ourselves in the church of Christ? When we read from the following passages, we gain a very different perspective of what and how Jesus pictured his bride, the church.

- John 13:34–35 and all of John 17
- Romans 12
- 1 Corinthians 12:12–13, 24–27
- Ephesians 4:1–7, 11–16

These passages teach us that Jesus sought to unify his disciples under the banner of God. He warned them that the world would hate us because of it, but that we should be in the world, not of it. These passages teach us that the church is the body of Christ and collectively that body should use its gifts to honor and glorify the Son and the Father. These passages teach that we should stand firm in our faith in times of joy as well as in times of suffering and adversity (as that faithfulness will be contrary to the world around us) so that we may all grow up and attain the entire fullness of God. We also learn together that though the world may ridicule us and encourage us to divide, we must love each other the same way Christ loved us. By this love all humankind will know we belong to Christ, and therefore, many will be drawn to that love. Indeed, we are admonished to live this way.

We are called to be more than fast-food Christians who belong to the Club of Christ. We must ask ourselves these questions:

- Am I a member of the Club of Christ or a member of the church of Christ?
- What example am I setting for those who worship with us?
- Would first-century disciples give up their lives for fast-food Christianity or for the Club of Christ? Would you?

We are called by Jesus to something greater. We are called by Jesus to follow him. But what does he mean by "follow me"? We have to answer that question candidly if we're ever going to share in the dynamic of D^2 discipleship.

52:7 and 52/7

In Mark 1:17, we hear Jesus call his first disciples by saying, "Follow me, and I will make you become fishers of men." Do we follow Jesus the way he intended for us to? If not, then why? Perhaps it is because we do not understand what it truly means to follow Jesus.

In the first century, to hear a rabbi say, "Follow me," was an extreme honor. An individual would have gone through years of study in the Bible as a child and adolescent. After that time, if a rabbi found someone who had an inclination to study God's Word further, then the rabbi would ask that individual to continue in his studies by following him (the rabbi) in his everyday walk to learn to become a rabbi. To do this meant to leave everything behind, choosing to follow the rabbi wherever he went. Why? In order that the individual might do what the rabbi did and to become who the rabbi was.

Those who didn't make the cut would go on to learn their father's trade and to join the family business. Peter, Andrew, James, and John were all fishermen by trade. They had, therefore, never heard the words "follow me" spoken to them by a rabbi. But when Jesus (a known rabbi) walked by and called to them, "Follow me," they dropped everything. Notice that even Zebedee, the father of James and John, did not question what they did or try to stop them (at least, from what we know). Perhaps Zebedee knew what an honor his sons had just been given. They were no longer the ones who "didn't make the cut."

Maybe we don't follow Jesus in the same way the early disciples did because we don't realize what an honor we have been given. None of us have "made the cut," but he calls us anyway. We should all be willing to leave everything behind to follow him. Yet too often we see people become "converts" and receive salvation without ever truly becoming disciples. Perhaps we have bought into the lie that Satan has taught us—the lie that says all we must do is "get saved" and that is enough, that we can be a fast-food Christian and belong to the Club of Christ and it's all good.

But it isn't "all good." We are called to something more, something greater. If we buy into Satan's lie, then all we do is cheapen God's grace and love given to us through Jesus, his only Son. This is called nominal Christianity: being a Christian in name and reaping the benefits but living an unchanged life. And that is a travesty.

Nominal Christianity is what Dietrich Bonhoeffer referred to as "cheap grace."[5] According to Bonhoeffer, this is grace that costs us nothing, and therefore we pay nothing. We receive this gift that cost God everything but give him little in return. Cheap grace recognizes that we have already received forgiveness, so we continue sinning, hide the sins, and simply go on living with little or no change in our lives. After all, we are saved, right? It is then that grace becomes a doctrine, a principle, or a system that we live by only when it suits our individual needs. Bonhoeffer says,

> The church that teaches this doctrine of grace thereby
> confers such grace upon itself. The world finds in this
> church a cheap cover-up for its sins, for which it shows
> no remorse and from which it has even less desire to
> be set free. Cheap grace is, thus, denial of God's living
> word, denial of the incarnation of the Word of God.[6]

He goes on to say that, "Cheap grace is grace without discipleship, grace without the cross, grace without the living, incarnate Jesus Christ."[7] May that never be.

I am convinced that there is more than being a fast-food Christian who is a member of the Club of Christ. I am convinced that Jesus has called us to follow him, to become his disciples, and to make other disciples (D^2). The culmination of that belief is found within the pages of this book. It is my desire that as you read it, you will become convinced—no, convicted—that God calls us to something greater. I hope you will be called to a higher calling given to you by God's grace through his Son, Jesus—that in the end, you will be willing to drop everything for the sake of Christ.

While I was sitting in a session at a conference, the speaker was focusing on the depths of discipleship. As he spoke, he called everyone to be a disciple 24/7 (living for Jesus twenty-four hours a day, seven days a week). But as he said those words, I was being challenged inside. Everything inside me screamed, "That's not enough!" I can easily live for Jesus for a day or a week, but how about every day through the next year? Could I commit to be a true disciple of Christ 52/7 (living for Jesus for fifty-two weeks, seven days a week)? When this hit me, I began to wonder if there were 52:7 passages in the Bible that speak about that type of commitment. So I opened my Bible to a couple of books that I knew had fifty-two chapters, and here is what I found.

The first book I opened to was Psalms. As I thumbed through the pages, I came to Psalm 52:7, and here is what I read: "See the man who would not make God his refuge, but trusted in the abundance of his riches and sought refuge in his own destruction!" I sat there thinking to myself, "Wow! This is where we all begin in our journey. We all begin with self-reliance and seek ourselves instead of God as our refuge." But I wondered if that was the only message God was teaching me. So I went to the next long book: Isaiah. Here's what I read in Isaiah 52:7: "How beautiful upon the mountains are the feet of him who brings good news, who publishes peace, who brings good news of happiness, who publishes salvation, who says to Zion, 'Your God reigns.'"

I sat there speechless. Now, you can sit there and say that it was all just a matter of chance, but I do not. I believe that God, in that moment of conviction, demonstrated to me the journey of discipleship from beginning to end. It is a journey that begins with self and ends with God. For as one starts by only relying on self, in the end (if we seek God with all our heart, soul, mind, and strength), we will fully rely on God as we bring good news to all the world shouting, "Your God reigns!" It is a 52:7 to 52/7 Journey of Discipleship. It is the sort of journey that Theodore Monod wrote about many years ago in the song "None of Self and All of Thee."

In this song, Monod takes the reader on a four-step journey toward Jesus. The first step, "All of self, and none of Thee," is when our pride is too great to truly claim Jesus as Lord of our lives. We cannot see beyond the end of our own noses to recognize the Savior, so it is all about us and nothing about him. The second step of the journey is "Some of self, and some of Thee." This is when we discover Jesus suffering on the cross on our behalf (or Jesus finds us, according to the song). It is here that our hearts begin to faintly and wistfully lean toward Jesus.

The third step is best understood by the author's own words:

Day by day His tender mercy,
Healing, helping, full and free,
Brought me lower while I whispered,
"Less of self, and more of Thee."

In this part of our journey, we are brought low and humbled before Jesus. Here, we place ourselves in his healing, helping hands, and he frees us from ourselves. Yet our journey is not over with this step. Why? Because we still have yet to give ourselves fully to him. We see him as the One who will grant us healing, forgiveness, and salvation, but we still feel comfortable holding back a portion of our self.

It is not until the fourth step, "None of self, and all of Thee," that we fully give Jesus all that we are. At this point, Jesus has fully conquered our self, and all that is left is our undivided, undistracted relationship with him. Oh, what a blessed day that will be! The day when all we see is Jesus and all we want is to be with him. This is the journey Jesus is calling us to. It is this 52:7 to 52/7 journey that Jesus calls us to as he cries out, "Follow me!"

It is not a journey we take to see what we can get out of it, but it is instead a journey we go on to see what we can pour into it. It is not a journey we go on to see what God will give us, but a journey we go on to see what we can give to God. Why? So that we can answer the honor of his call: the call to become his disciple, his child—the call to become the disciple of the Lord of *all,* the God who created all things, sustains all things, and rules all things.

I am no longer content with drawing people to fast-food Christianity so that they can become members of our Club of Christ. Instead, I am convinced that we must choose to become part of God's story of redemption and answer his call to be disciples who make disciples for the sake and honor of Jesus Christ. Will you join me in this privilege to live as disciples of Christ? That is what this book is all about. I want not only to share with you the importance of discipleship and why it is the mission of Christ, but also to help you understand how to develop a plan for discipleship in your own life.

It is a 52/7 journey. I am challenging you to use this next year to commit to being a disciple of Christ for fifty-two weeks, seven days a week. I will provide help and guidance toward this goal in the following pages. I want to provide you as much support as I can to live your part in God's story of redemption. He is calling you, saying, "Follow me!" Will you join him and answer his call?

Hopefully, the pages that follow will help you understand what I believe Scripture teaches us about discipleship and how we are to live it out. I know the plan I am suggesting is not perfect. Only he whom I follow is perfect. My goal is to provide you with some beginning steps toward this goal. Remember: our journey in discipleship is usually not in leaps and bounds (although those may occur at times), but in small, intentional steps taken daily for the love of Jesus Christ, through the power of the Holy Spirit, and for the glory and praise of God the Father. These pages are filled with my journey of discovery. This journey has been taking place over many years, and I have learned many things (and will continue to do so). However, I believe that we can't tarry any longer and wait for something perfect. Instead, we need to move forward, following the One who is perfect and trusting that he will lead us on the path.

Fellowship of the Unashamed

This letter was found in the office of a young minister in Zimbabwe, Africa, following his martyrdom for Christ.

I'm part of the fellowship of the unashamed. I have the Holy Spirit power. The die has been cast. I have stepped over the line. The decision has been made—I'm a disciple of His. I won't look back, let up, slow down, back away, or be still. My past is redeemed, my present makes sense, my future is secure. I'm finished and done with low living, sight walking, smooth knees, colorless dreams, tamed visions, worldly talking, cheap giving, and dwarfed goals.

I no longer need preeminence, prosperity, position, promotions, plaudits, or popularity. I don't have to be right, first, tops, recognized, praised, regarded, or rewarded. I now live by faith, lean on His presence, walk by patience, am uplifted by prayer, and I labor with power.

My face is set, my gait is fast, my goal is heaven, my road is narrow, my way rough, my companions are few, my Guide reliable, my mission clear. I cannot be bought, compromised, detoured, lured away, turned back, deluded, or delayed. I will not flinch in the face of sacrifice, hesitate in the presence of the enemy, pander at the pool of popularity, or meander in the maze of mediocrity.

I won't give up, shut up, let up, until I have stayed up, stored up, prayed up, paid up, preached up for the cause of Christ. I am a disciple of Jesus. I must go till He comes, give till I drop, preach till all know, and work till He stops me. And, when He comes for His own, He will have no problem recognizing me . . . my banner will be clear![8]

I call you to join me in this journey. If you are satisfied with a fast-food Christianity and with being a member of the Club of Christ, then you may not like what I have to share. In fact, you will most likely complain and/or look for holes in the plan to keep from joining. However, if you are no longer satisfied with where you have been but are ready to live fully in the life God has called you to, then keep reading, learning, growing, and living your journey of discipleship with me. Will you join the journey?

Before I move on though, and before you make this commitment, I ask that you commit to being a part of the "Fellowship of the Unashamed." I want our journey together to start with a commitment to and with God. But be careful! When you make such a commitment, God expects that you will follow through. Don't make the commitment if you don't mean the words.

If you are ready to make the commitment to true discipleship, then let's start the 52:7 to 52/7 journey.

Two Truths—D²

"We hold these truths to be self-evident." When the founding fathers of the United States wanted to be free from the tyranny and oppression of the British monarchy, they penned (on pain of death for treason) the Declaration of Independence. They were convicted that the colonies should separate from the rule and power of another nation to claim freedom for those who could not claim it for themselves. Through that conviction, they wrote:

> When in the Course of human events it becomes necessary for one people to dissolve the political bands which have connected them with another and to assume among the powers of the earth, the separate and equal station to which the Laws of Nature and of Nature's God entitle them, a decent respect to the opinions of

mankind requires that they should declare the causes
which impel them to the separation.

Why is this important? A ruling power exists in this world that
we often ignore. In fact, this rule and authority is unseen: "We do
not wrestle against flesh and blood, but against the rulers, against
the authorities, against the cosmic powers over the present darkness, against the spiritual forces of evil in the heavenly places"
(Eph. 6:12). It is an oppressive and tyrannical rule that seeks nothing else but to enslave all humanity.

Yet this rule is deceptive and often promises to satisfy every
human desire if one will just relinquish their soul. Take note, the
ruler of this governing power is a tyrant. He cares nothing for those
he rules over and wants nothing more than to devour them (1 Pet.
5:8). He cares for nothing or no one but himself. However, people
are drawn to him as he deceives them and promises them great
things. In fact, he blinds the eyes of people who do not believe so
that they cannot see the light and glory of freedom found only
through Jesus (2 Cor. 4:4). Instead, those individuals follow the
course of the ruling authority in this world, the prince of the power
of the air, who, as Paul says in Ephesians 2:2, is at work in those of
disobedience (who seek only to gratify the god of "self").

The interesting thing is that we do not have to live under this
rule. Like the freedom that is treasured in the United States, it has
been bought with blood. Not by the blood of many, but by the
blood of one—one who came to fight for us, to claim victory for us,
and to pronounce for us freedom from the tyrannical rule of sin
and its ruler, Satan. Jesus, our victor, calls us to live a victorious life
through him. He asks us all to make a declaration of dependence
on him. A declaration that may be confessed and lived on pain
of death and suffering. A declaration that might echo America's
colonial leaders by proclaiming:

> When in the Course of the history of salvation, it
> becomes necessary for the unified people of God to dis-
> solve the bonds of sin which have connected them with
> the world and separated them from God, a reverence to
> the redemption, bought by the blood of Christ, requires
> that they should declare the causes which urge them to
> the separation.

This declaration of dependence on Christ urges us toward truth that is found only in Jesus. As our founding fathers declared certain truths to be self-evident, today we hold this truth to be self-evident: Jesus *is* the way, the truth, and the life. No one can go to the Father except through him (John 14:6). This truth leads us to recognize two additional, irrefutable, self-evident truths regarding every human being: (1) we are always being discipled and (2) discipling someone to Jesus.

We always have someone (or even something) influencing us toward a certain path in life. This influence can come through media (that may be discipling us toward self-fulfillment, self-worth, and self-confidence), parents (who are discipling us toward success, achievement, and fulfillment), or friends (who may disciple us toward their interests). The point is that we have individuals (or influencing messages, such as media, governments, philosophies, ideologies, and others) in our lives who are helping shape us into the people we are and will become. Those individuals are led either by the Spirit of God or by the spirit of the prince of this world. It is our job to discern which one.

The same can be said of the second point: we are always discipling someone. We may not be aware of that person, and they may never let us know the influence we are having on their life, but we are nonetheless discipling them. We are making a direct impact on the way others live and the choices they make, for good (through the Spirit of God) or bad (through the spirit of the prince of this world). Each of us pulls from the available pool of resources (most of the time through relationships) to grow and to become the people we want to be.

The question, then, is not an "if" but "who?" That is: (1) who (or even what) is discipling me? and (2) whom am I discipling? The answers to those two questions help us discover the impact others have on us and the impact we are having on them. As Christians, having made the declaration of dependence on Christ, our desire is to follow our leader, who calls us to fulfill the Great Commission Jesus gives us in Matthew 28:18–20: "All authority in heaven and on earth has been given to me. Go therefore and make disciples of all nations, baptizing them in the name of the Father and of the Son and of the Holy Spirit, teaching them to observe all that I have commanded you. And behold, I am with you always, to the end of the age."

This command from Jesus before his ascension to heaven is known to be one of the primary tasks of all Christ-followers (disciples). Yet this was not the first time it was uttered by God. What? You heard me. Jesus did not first speak the Great Commission prior to his ascension. He also uttered it in the beginning with God.

The First Great Commission

In Genesis 1 we read of the creation account. Verses 26–27 tell of the creation of humans:

> Then God said, "Let us make man in our image, after
> our likeness. And let them have dominion over the fish
> of the sea and over the birds of the heavens and over the
> livestock and over all the earth and over every creep-
> ing thing that creeps on the earth." So God created man

in his own image, in the image of God he created him;
male and female he created them.

When God creates man and woman in his image (the *imago Dei*),
he gives them dominion over the earth. However, dominion was
not the only task he gave us.

In 1:28, God tells his children, "Be fruitful and multiply and
fill the earth and subdue it," and then he repeats his call for them
to have dominion over it. His instruction to "be fruitful and
multiply and fill the earth" occurs often in Genesis (see 9:1, 7;
17:1–8; 26:4; 35:11; 48:4). It was God's intention from the beginning for his created children to go out and make more children.
Why? Because this is how he created them. You see, God created
all things, but when he got to the creation of man, the process
changed. Something was different about how he created man and
woman. What was it? He created man and woman in his *image* and
likeness, unlike all the rest of creation. This unique characteristic
of humans is what God wanted to be multiplied throughout the
earth. Why? Well, let's take a closer look.

The Representation of God

Those two Hebrew words that surface in Genesis 1:26–27 have
been a topic of discussion through the years. The terms "image"
(*tselem*) and "likeness" (*demût*), when referring to the creation of
humans, occur in only three passages (Gen. 1:26–27; 5:1–3; and
9:6). The terms represent relationality between God and humankind. Out of God's great love, he created man and woman in his
likeness and image. Therefore, we are intimately connected with
God in our very DNA (so to speak).

Yet why the use of two separate terms? Do they mean the same
thing, or do they have different meanings? While others have
argued for a distinction, I tend to agree with Wayne Grudem and

Anthony Hoekema, who say there is only a slight difference in the words. They demonstrate that the two basically synonymous words are used together to emphasize the point that humankind was created *as a representation of God* and *to be like God in certain aspects.*[1] In his commentary on Genesis, Kenneth Mathews agrees with the synonymous and interchangeable interpretation, but he adds that image and likeness are better defined as physical representations. He believes that others have been wrong to push the view that the *imago Dei* is either physical or spiritual. Instead, he says, the Hebrews would view man as a whole (not simply the mind or spirit or body) and that we humans represent God in whole—we are his image and likeness both physically and spiritually.[2]

If you think about it, we are God's representations on earth. Our physical representation of God would be similar to statues or drawings that depict someone or something. Think about the statues of rulers you have seen. Those statues were made and distributed across a ruler's territory to show who the governing authority of the land was. Wherever the statue sat was the area the ruler controlled. So the image represented the rule. One modern way to view this is when someone is saving a seat. How do they do it? They usually put something in the seat that represents the person who will occupy it. So, since the person is not there, whatever they have put in the seat (such as a coat or purse) represents that person and their ownership.

Even Jesus addressed this issue when he was asked if taxes should be paid to Caesar. Jesus said in Matthew 22:19–21, "'Show me the coin for the tax.' And they brought him a denarius. And Jesus said to them, 'Whose likeness and inscription is this?' They said, 'Caesar's.' Then he said to them, 'Therefore render to Caesar the things that are Caesar's, and to God the things that are God's.'" Jesus was telling them to give the coins to Caesar. They belonged to him because his image was firmly stamped on them. However, Jesus was making an even bigger statement here, because he then told them to give to God what is God's. He was telling them that they were firmly stamped in the image of God and, therefore, they should fully devote themselves (holy and wholly) to God.

These examples help us understand that God intended an intimate relationship with human beings from the beginning. Humans share a unique attachment with God that no plant, animal, or object enjoys. This unique privilege places in each of us an innate longing for and connection to the Father, just as Jesus demonstrated. We are connected to God and he to us through our very existence. The way that we were created means that by God's design, we represent and reflect him wherever we are. This is what we are to go and multiply: God's image and likeness.

Let's consider this in light of several passages of Scripture.

In Genesis 5:1–3, for example, we are reminded, "When God created man, he made him *in the likeness of God*. Male and female he created them, and he blessed them and named them Man when they were created" (emphasis added). This passage goes on to tell us that Adam fathered his own son after his own image and likeness. So the image of God was passed on from father to son. This "image reproduction process" has happened since the beginning. This is how God fills the earth with his image and likeness: with human representations of God.

We also find God commanding humankind explicitly to not create or make any image or likeness of him or of anything in heaven or on earth (Ex. 20:4; Lev. 26:1). This is important, as it connects with the command to make more images and likenesses of God through procreation, with the prohibition of human-made, hand-carved images. Why is this a big deal to God? Well, think about it. One image and likeness is created by God's hand, the other by human hands. If we resort to our own imaginations, we will create our own gods instead of worshiping the one true God. The gods we create will always resemble ourselves and our own passions and desires rather than God and his passions and desires.

The New Testament picks up on this concept by clarifying what the image is that we are to become. Yes, it is the image of God, but in the form of his Son, Jesus Christ. One immediately recognizes that much of what is discussed about the image of God in the New Testament is connected to Jesus Christ and conformity to his image. The first passage often mentioned is James 3:9: "With it [the tongue] we bless our Lord and Father, and with it we curse people who are made in the likeness of God." James considers the image of God something humans still reflect. The passage does not tell us what exactly the image of God is, how sin affects it, or what happens to it when it is recreated in us. What it does say is that it has not been completely destroyed and still exists in us in some fashion.

In his letters, Paul shares several thoughts about the image of God. In 2 Corinthians 4:4 we read, "In their case the god of this world has blinded the minds of the unbelievers, to keep them from seeing the light of the gospel of the glory of Christ, *who is the image of God*" (emphasis added). In verse six, we find that the knowledge of the glory of God is understood only in the face of Christ. In other words, when we see Christ, we see God. This is also affirmed when Paul tells the Colossians that Jesus is the image of the invisible God (1:15). The writer of Hebrews agrees with Paul by saying in Hebrew 1:3, "He is the radiance of the glory of God and the exact imprint of his nature." Once again, when we see Christ, we are looking at the invisible God made visible.

Paul also tells us in Colossians 3:9–10 that when anyone gives themselves over to Christ, they become a "new self" that is being renewed in the image of God. He goes on to tell the Ephesians that we are essentially taking off our old clothes (stained and unclean) and putting on new clothes, cleansed through the blood of Jesus. When we do this, we are being renewed in the image of God through Jesus and reflect/represent him and his glory. He says in Ephesians 4:20–24,

> That is not the way you learned Christ!—assuming that you have heard about him and were taught in him, as the truth is in Jesus, to put off your old self, which belongs to your former manner of life and is corrupt through deceitful desires, and to be renewed in the spirit of your minds, and to put on the new self, *created after the likeness of God* in true righteousness and holiness. (emphasis added)

According to Paul, we are in a continual state of being conformed and transformed into this image. He says in Romans 8:29, "Those whom he foreknew he also predestined *to be conformed to the image of his Son*, in order that he might be the firstborn among many brothers."

These passages teach that redemption is gained in and through Jesus Christ, and he, through the presence of his Spirit within us, is renewing and transforming humankind more and more into the image of God. Why? To save us and to fill the earth with his image, his representation. It is important to note that the image of God is not something that is static, but dynamic and moving God's children toward the goal of returning to his presence forever. It is a process that is taking place in each child of God daily. It is also something that cannot be renewed without the work of God through his Son and the Holy Spirit. Yet it requires action from us. We still have a responsibility in the work of renewal.

What can we take away from all these passages? It is important for us to realize that we have the honor of being created by God in his likeness and image. This is a privilege not extended to the rest of creation. As his special creation, we are the object of his love and endowed with specific roles and responsibilities, which we should take very seriously in order to honor and glorify God.

The scriptures we've just looked at also demonstrate that as we multiply (both in a physical and a spiritual sense), we are creating more images of God. Adam created Seth in his image and likeness, which is the image and likeness of God. That means the image is passed along from one person to the next, which is why God is so jealous and does not want us to have any idols carved in any image or likeness. Why? Because *we* are his image and likeness and *we* are supposed to represent and reflect him in this world. Nothing else in all of creation can compare. Romans 8:29 says that this was God's plan before creation. He wanted us to be conformed to the image of his Son, Jesus (who is the *imago Dei*).

Does all that make sense? As you were created, so you are to "go and multiply." So when we have children both physically and spiritually, we are being fruitful and multiplying the image of God, which is the image of Christ. From a spiritual sense, when we become a Christian, God begins to restore the image he created us in but that we distorted because of our sin. So every day, the Holy Spirit is working to form, conform, and transform us into the image of Christ. Then, as we go and make disciples, we are multiplying the image of God throughout the earth.

This was the mission of Christ, and therefore, it is our mission. If we accept Jesus's call to "follow me" and declare our state of dependence on him, then we are called to live out his mission on earth as if he were living it through us. So we must be diligent to know not only the words of the Great Commission, but also how to obey them. Through Jesus's words, we discover four words of action: go, make, baptize, and teach (disciples). But what do the words mean for us?

Go and make. The Great Commission tells us to go and make disciples. This means that we must pursue the lost and help them in the process of becoming disciples of Jesus. It means that we cannot grow comfortable in our pews but are instead called to stand up and go out. Our job as disciples of Christ is to help the lost accept Jesus as their Lord and Savior and to prepare them to spread his message and love to others. But how do we go and do this? The Great Commission tells us two ways.

Baptize. We have often confused baptism with being the Great Commission itself. Baptism is the *how*, not the *commission*. What is the purpose of baptism? Baptism allows us to personally participate in the gospel message: the death, burial, and resurrection of Jesus (Rom. 6:3–8). Baptism is an expression of our faith in Jesus, and it identifies us as believers who share in the person and work of Jesus Christ (Gal. 3:26–27). At baptism, we receive the forgiveness of sins and the gift of the Holy Spirit (Acts 2:38).

Now, some will argue those points. However, I believe that Scripture indicates that baptism fulfills these things. A question often arises: "Is baptism necessary for salvation?" The best response I have is this: salvation belongs to our God. When and how it happens is up to him. We simply want to be faithful to his commands. However, baptism is necessary for discipleship. Why? Because Jesus said so. If you don't believe this, then read the Great Commission again. But here's the deal. We are not done in discipling others when they repent of their sins, confess Christ Jesus, accept him as their Lord and Savior, and are baptized into him. At that point, the journey is actually just beginning. Our role in discipleship continues, and the Great Commission tells us how.

Teach. To simply baptize someone leaves the job of discipling only partially done. The second *how* to the Great Commission is to *teach*. We must teach those we baptize what the commitment of discipleship means. To teach means to equip believers to be active in their faith through serving God. But what does it mean to equip others? The online Merriam-Webster dictionary gives the following definitions: "to furnish for service or action by appropriate provisioning, to make ready: prepare." If this is true, then how do we equip new disciples of Christ? We can do so in three ways:

1. Teach them that being a Christian is an everyday commitment (Matt. 16:24; Mark 8:34; Luke 9:23; 14:26–27; 14:33).
2. Teach them that part of that commitment to Christ is a commitment to his body (church/family). That means they must be active participants in the family (1 Cor. 12:12–13; Eph. 2:19–22; 4:1–16).
3. Teach them the necessary skills for spreading God's love (that is, relationships, knowledge of God's Word, love, and other skills).

Those four words of action—go, make, baptize, and teach—will push us toward fulfilling the Great Commission. While understanding the definitions helps us understand the action we need to take, they can often leave us wondering what is at the core of Christ's mission. Our mission for discipleship needs to be clear so that everyone in the Christian fellowship will work together toward a common purpose. This leads us to a shared mission for discipleship.

With this in mind, I want the D² concept (disciples making disciples) to challenge all of us to allow God's Spirit and his Word to infiltrate all areas of life and ministry as a guide and filter toward our becoming devoted followers (disciples) of Jesus Christ who in turn win others to our Lord. I recognize that as humans we will often fail at this, but I trust in God and his ability to lead us in these efforts. As Paul said to the Colossians, we toil and struggle with the energy and power of Christ within us "that we may present everyone mature in Christ" and "that you may stand mature, and fully assured in all the will of God" (Col. 1:28 and 4:12). I only wish that he alone may receive all glory and honor and that we as the family of God are recognized simply as his children who love and follow him as we live out his mission on earth.

In the coming chapters, you will find information concerning how we can live out our declaration of dependence on Christ and God's mission for discipleship as I believe the Lord revealed it. I am confident of his revelation and recognize that he may continue to adapt it as he grows us and leads us ever closer to him. In the following chapters, I will look at how to be a disciple and how to disciple others so that we may all become more like Jesus (little Christs) every day. More specifically, you will discover how to make a personalized plan toward discipleship for yourself and for others.

Chapter 3

Untangling Discipleship

I began this journey in discipleship and spiritual formation through prayer and study and by asking some very specific questions:

What is spiritual maturity?

What is a disciple?

What is discipleship or discipling?

What is spiritual growth or formation?

I discovered quickly that many differing answers are offered to those questions. While some may disagree with the following explanations and definitions, these will be the definitions I use as a frame of reference throughout this book.

What Is Spiritual Maturity?

While considering this question, my discipleship team and I spent several weeks studying the different passages in the Bible that speak about spiritual maturity. We discovered several passages that discuss maturing in our faith, such as Hebrews 5:12–6:2. Here, the author rebukes his readers for their lack of spiritual maturity. Using potent wording, he tells them they are still babies in their faith when they should be spiritual adults. He is essentially scolding them.

He tells them they are "dull of hearing" (which means they are sluggish—6:12) and content with where they are. It appears they have lost the reverence and awe for who Christ is, what he has done for them, and how they should live and mature in faith and hope. To drive the point even more, the author uses the metaphor of food and how it nourishes and helps us grow. The food we eat changes as we grow older. It is the same with our spiritual growth process. As we grow, our spiritual food is supposed to become more substantial, which ultimately helps us discern between good and evil. He goes on to say in Hebrews 6:1, "Therefore let us leave the elementary doctrine of Christ and go on to maturity."

Another passage that speaks about spiritual maturity is Colossians 1:24–29, where Paul describes his ministry to the church. Here, Paul discusses how he was called to make God's Word fully known by showing how the long-held mystery of salvation has now been revealed through Jesus, who is now in each of them through the presence of the Holy Spirit. He tells the Colossians that he is toiling and struggling to warn and teach everyone the hope of glory found only through Christ. But, why does he toil, struggle, and suffer to teach the Word of God? He tells his Colossian converts he did it so "that we may present everyone mature in Christ." Paul's greatest aim in ministry was to walk alongside others so that they might be mature in their faith when he stands with them before God.

One other passage that my team focused on in our studies was Ephesians 4:11–16. We spent a great deal of time with this passage, and I believe it needs to be read in full here, since it speaks deeply about spiritual maturity:

> He gave the apostles, the prophets, the evangelists, the shepherds and teachers, to equip the saints for the work of ministry, for building up the body of Christ, until we all attain to the unity of the faith and of the knowledge of the Son of God, to mature manhood, to the measure of the stature of the fullness of Christ, so that we may no longer be children, tossed to and fro by the waves and carried about by every wind of doctrine, by human cunning, by craftiness in deceitful schemes. Rather, speaking the truth in love, we are to grow up in every way into him who is the head, into Christ, from whom the whole body, joined and held together by every joint with which it is equipped, when each part is working properly, makes the body grow so that it builds itself up in love.

In this passage, Paul defines our ministry to the church as helping family members grow up in Christ. This spiritual maturity allows us to be filled with the Spirit to the "fullness of Christ." Why do we need this? Without it, we will be tossed back and forth from one philosophy or worldly teaching to another. We will struggle with knowing the difference between God's truth and man's. This will result in us being led in two different directions without ever really going anywhere.

This reminds me of the Dr. Suess poem called "The Zode." The Zode is caught between making a decision to go one direction or another. After a great deal of mental gymnastics in order to decide which road to take, the Zode decides: "Then he got an idea that was wonderfully bright! 'Play safe!' cried the Zode. 'I'll play safe. I'm no dunce! I'll simply start out for both places at once!' And that's how the Zode who would not take a chance got no place at all with a split in his pants."

And that is what we will do with our spiritual lives if we are not careful. We will be tossed from human ideologies to the truth of God without ever making a movement toward God in spiritual maturity. Instead, Paul encourages the Ephesians to take a chance and work toward maturity in Christ. The purpose for this, he said, was so that the body of Christ might grow and mature in love and righteousness. This should also be our goal both individually and as a Christian family.

These are but a few of the passages we found that highlight spiritual maturity. Through them, we discovered that spiritual maturity is attained as we grow in our knowledge of God's Word. Yet this is more than simple head-knowledge; it is a practical living-out of the knowledge of God's Word in everyday life. It is being the living word of God. From those passages, we determined that spiritual maturity is an ever-increasing ability to apply God's Word to life.

Note that it is "ever-increasing." None of us will have a full knowledge of God's Word in this life, but we should strive each day to know God more through his Word. The more we strive for this, the more we grow. The more we grow, the more we live out that knowledge daily for his glory and not our own. I believe that spiritual maturity is evident in an individual when one's faith:

- Serves as the catalyst for how and why one thinks about things.
- Creates the lens through which life is seen (2 Cor. 4:18; Eph. 1:17–23).
- Motivates and shapes thinking (Rom. 12:1–2; 1 Cor. 2:10–16; Heb. 3:1).

- Provides the means and focal point for "centering" oneself.
- Gives certainty in an uncertain world, surety when life is anything but sure (Luke 1:3–4; John 17:8; Heb. 11:1).
- Provides the ability to weather life's storms and experience joy (Matt. 11:28–30; 2 Cor. 4:7–12, 16–17).
- Defines one's interaction with others.
- Encourages one to recognize and respond to needs (Gal. 6:10; Phil. 2:1–4; 1 John 3:18).
- Motivates one to be supportive and to build up others (Eph. 4:11–16).
- Causes Christ-like behavior and attitude in our love, concern, care, and compassion (Eph. 4:29–5:2).
- Defines and shapes how one deals with the world (John 17:13–19; Rom. 12:1–2).

We are all called, as disciples of Christ, to grow toward spiritual maturity. We are called to come to know God through his Word and to live out that Word each day. But, if we're truly committed to the principles of D²—of becoming and making real disciples of Jesus—then we need to seriously ask: What exactly is a disciple?

What Is a Disciple?

I discovered many definitions for "disciple." As I noted in Chapter One, there is a big difference in being a convert and being a disciple of Christ. I knew there was something more than being a fast-food Christian who belonged to the Club of Christ. Are we satisfied with simply becoming believers in Jesus (or what the Bible calls "the crowd")? Or do we want to walk down the path of becoming true disciples of Christ?

A general (even worldly) definition of a disciple is "a committed follower of a great master." However, a more specific definition for us Christians is: "A disciple of Jesus is one who has come to Jesus for eternal life, has claimed Jesus as Savior and God, and has embarked upon the life of following Jesus."[1] So a disciple is one who demonstrates the ever-increasing characteristics of spiritual maturity as the Spirit of Christ dwells in them and is transforming them into his image, but there is so much more to the definition than this. There is a marked difference between believing that Jesus saves you (the crowd) and truly following him (a disciple). This will take some further explanation.

The Crowd

Often, in the Gospels we see Jesus addressing "the crowd." Several passages report that "great crowds followed him" (Matt. 4:25; 8:1; 13:2). Often, the crowd was big. They came out to hear the teachings of a great rabbi who they had heard did great and wonderful things. They wanted to hear his words and witness (or participate in) his signs. Yet these individuals had not made a commitment to Jesus. Instead, they were simply coming out to hear a great sermon and perhaps be fed, healed, or more. They came to get their needs met, but many left unchanged.

One of the greatest examples of this is found in Matthew 13. Verse 2 says, "Great crowds gathered about him." So much so that Jesus had to get into a boat and push out a bit from the shore to address this large group of people. There, he shared the parable of the sower. As recorded in Matthew, it's a pretty short sermon. Jesus gets the message out there and says, "He who has ears, let him hear," and then he is done. I often think that people would love for Jesus to preach each Sunday. They could listen to the sermon and get out of the worship service in about 5 minutes. That's the problem. The crowd is always looking for a quick sermon with a great point and good stories. They are looking for something that will tug at their heartstrings but allow them to quickly move on to the rest of their agenda.

They go away saying, "Great sermon! I was really moved this morning." Unfortunately, they weren't. Although they may have been emotionally moved, they were not moved toward living Christ in everyday life. As Eric Geiger, Michael Kelley, and Philip Nation note, "The sad reality is that the daily lives, aspirations, and desires of many people in our churches mirror those who do not claim to know Christ."[2] Jim Putman, Bobby Harrington William, and Robert Coleman describe the difference between being a Christian and being a disciple:

> One problem today is that churches are full of
> "Christians" but not disciples, and yes, there is a signifi-
> cant difference. In the early church, the first followers
> of Jesus were called disciples. Later they were called
> Christians because of their association with Christ
> (Acts 11:26). But the Bible never instructs us to make
> Christians, not in today's loose sense of the word.[3]

So if we're really serious about fulfilling our Lord's D² imperatives, we need to ask seriously if it is possible to be a Christian without being a disciple. That's what Jesus is addressing in Matthew 13 with the parable of the sower. It's called the parable of the sower based on verse 18, but it may be more consistent to call it the parable of the soils. Why? In the parable, Jesus is specifically addressing the receptivity to his message about repentance and the kingdom of heaven. He is challenging his hearers about what they are doing with the message they receive from him.

Although no particular identification of the sower is given here, it is assumed that the sower is Jesus, since he states in verse 37, "The one who sows the good seed is the Son of Man." However, it could also refer to anyone who shares the gospel message of

Jesus. As the seed of Jesus's gospel message is being sown, it lands on different soils. The soil is our hearing and our receiving or understanding. It is our faith.

Simply having knowledge about a particular topic (in this instance, the gospel message of Jesus) does not mean an internal change has been made that brings about action. The first step is to gain the knowledge (a matter of the head). This knowledge is what Jesus means by "hear" in the parable. Hearing the message means that it enters the head or mind. But then the longest journey begins, and Jesus refers to it as "receiving" or "understanding." This understanding is the journey from the head to the heart—only twelve inches. That twelve-inch journey is going deeper with the knowledge to the point that we understand it.

Jesus refers to the final step as "bearing fruit." Those who not only hear the word and receive or understand it but also put it into action are moving from knowledge and understanding to wisdom. This movement is demonstrated through an individual's actions. It is the fruit they bear. When one takes what they know and understand and put it into practice, then they demonstrate godly wisdom, moving from head to heart to hands.[4]

Jesus goes on in his parable to share the four different types of soil that receive his gospel message. All of us fall into one of these four categories, and we often fluctuate between them. Let's take a closer look at the first three soils, as they represent those who are a part of the crowd.

- **The path**—The first soil is the path. The seed is thrown out on the path where people walk. There, the soil has been walked on so much that it has become hard. Therefore, the seed does not go deep into the ground (heart), which allows the birds to swoop down and take it away. Jesus explains this by saying, "When anyone hears the word of the kingdom and does not understand it, the evil one comes and snatches away what has been sown in his heart. This is what was sown along the path" (Matt. 13:19).

- **The rocks**—The rocky soil does not have a great deal of actual soil. Instead, it is filled with rocks that keep the seed from taking root. This person hears the message of Jesus and gladly and joyfully receives it. However, it doesn't go any deeper than the crowding rocks allow it to. Those rocks are the struggles and difficulties we face in life. As Jesus explains, "As for what was sown on rocky ground, this is the one who hears the word and immediately receives it with joy, yet he has no root in himself, but endures for a while, and when tribulation or persecution arises on account of the word, immediately he falls away" (13:20–21).

- **The thorns**—The soil filled with thorns crowds out the ability of the seed to grow a fruitful plant. Instead, the weeds and thorns surround the budding plant. It grows, but it bears no fruit. This person hears the word and permits it to take root in the heart, but then allows the cares of the world to become overwhelming. Therefore, the word cannot bear fruit. Jesus describes this soil by saying, "As for what was sown among thorns, this is the one who hears the word, but the cares of the world and the deceitfulness of riches choke the word, and it proves unfruitful" (13:22).

In describing these three soils, Jesus is actually describing the crowd. The people come out to hear his message. Some hear it, and the message is quickly taken away from them. Others hear the message, but it takes no root. And still others hear it and understand it, but they are more concerned with the things of the world than the things of God. Therefore, they do not end up putting anything into action. Instead, they sit in pews and discuss Jesus rather than going out and living as he would. These soils could not be described as disciples. Do you fall into one of these three categories? Or do you see yourself being described as the good soil (soil that demonstrates the life of a disciple)? Let's take a look at what this means.

The Disciples

Jesus says, "As for what was sown on good soil, this is the one who hears the word and understands it. He indeed bears fruit and yields, in one case a hundredfold, in another sixty, and in another thirty" (13:23). Disciples are different from the crowd. True disciples hear the message and not only ask, "What does that even mean?" but also, "What must I do to live it?" In other words, genuine disciples are not satisfied with a surface message, a surface relationship, or a surface life. They want to go deeper, know more, live more, and be known more by the One they follow.

A disciple could also be defined as an apprentice—someone who decides to be with another person to learn to do what that person *does* or to become who that person *is*. But this comes into sharp contrast with worldly expectations that say you are your own person or individual. "You be you," the world would tell us. Yet a disciple of Christ is someone who is learning from Christ how to live his or her life in the way Christ would live that life if he were that person. So how would Christ live your life if he were living it?

Dallas Willard spent much of his life trying to define what it means to be a disciple and how to become one. To him, being a disciple of Jesus is something quite evident. Nobody should have to guess if you are one or not, and it should be quite evident to you as well. As Willard says, "First of all, we should note that being a disciple, or apprentice, of Jesus is a quite definite and obvious kind of thing. To make a mystery of it is to misunderstand it. There is no good reason why people should ever be in doubt as to whether they themselves are his students or not."[5]

To become a disciple, Willard goes on to say, is to decide to be with another person "in order to become capable of doing what that person does or to become what that person is."[6] To be a disciple of Jesus, I choose to be with him (since he has extended his grace to me) and to learn from him how to live in God's kingdom here on earth.

To live in God's kingdom on earth means that we live within the will of God and allow the life of Jesus to flow through ours. As Dallas Willard puts it, "I am learning from Jesus to live my life as he would live my life if he were I. I am not necessarily learning to do everything he did, but I am learning how to do everything I do in the manner that he did all that he did."[7] By this, we come to understand that the whole of our lives is connected with our "apprenticeship" with Jesus. So there should be no part-time Christians. That's the fast-food, Club of Christ mentality I addressed earlier.

Instead, I focus my daily living as a disciple on learning how to live my life as Jesus would live it. This is not living Jesus's life. We don't need to do that, because Jesus already lived it. Besides, there's no way we could ever do it, because we are not Jesus. However, we can strive to live our lives as if Jesus got inside our skins and were living them for us. Which, of course, is exactly what his Spirit is supposed to be doing. Jesus sent his Spirit to live inside us to enable us to live our lives according to his Spirit, not our own. He did this because he loves us and is interested in our lives and not disconnected from them. As Willard says, "There lies my need. I need to be able to lead my life as he would lead it if he were I."[8]

This picture is very different from what we often think is required of us as Christians. After all, isn't the gospel about Jesus saving us from our sins so that we can be in heaven? Yet a life lived with that mindset and attitude is one that focuses on salvation being for us, rather than on how salvation is about him. When we begin to truly grasp the depths of what God did for us through his Son, we cannot help but desire to live a life that is in praise and thanksgiving to God for his gift and his tremendous display of love. Too many of us are often completely satisfied with receiving God's grace with little to no regard for giving it. We desire to gain all the privileges of a disciple minus the necessary commitment to be one.

Bill Hull, in his book *The Complete Book of Discipleship,* says that the struggle we have with being a true disciple has to do with interference. He says, "Interference occurs when someone sticks his nose in your business. However, that's precisely what discipleship is all about. If you want to grow in a meaningful way, you not only must tolerate another person's intimate knowledge of you, you must also willingly invite that person into your life."[9] Often, we don't want this sort of "interference" because we would rather enjoy the benefits of being a Christian (receive grace, mercy, forgiveness, and God's love) while living life as we would choose to live it: for ourselves. As Hull says, "We want all the benefits of humility and growth without being humble or working to grow."[10] But the Bible tells us over and over that interference is exactly what we need in order to keep us from leading self-focused lives.

This interference that Jesus uses makes us squeamish about being a real disciple, as opposed to just being a part of the crowd and enjoying all the benefits. We discussed this nominal Christianity (being a Christian in name and reaping the benefits, but living an unchanged life) in Chapter One. If we are to be disciples who sit at the feet of and follow close behind our rabbi, then we must be willing to allow him to interfere in our lives and to challenge us where we are most unlike him. This is not really interference. This is *love*! As disciples, we make a commitment to allow Jesus to interfere and grow us.

To be a true disciple we must: (1) come after Jesus, (2) deny ourselves, (3) take up our cross (accept suffering and rejection) daily, and *then* (4) follow him (Luke 9:23). We like to skip steps 1 to 3 and go straight to step 4 and say we are okay. But Jesus requires that we start at step 1 and then proceed to step 4. This is the ongoing process of growth as a disciple that is accurately called discipleship.[11]

What Is Discipleship?

We all willingly enter this process of discipleship to become more like Jesus and to live our lives as if he were living them for us. Yet we may wonder what is meant by the term "discipleship." This word is not found in the Bible, but the concept is addressed. We hear it all the time, but what is it? Well, know with certainty that it is not a program in the church or an offset ministry limited to those who are "gifted" for it. Discipleship is not a ministry in the church, it is the ministry of the church. As Hull says, "Discipleship isn't a program or an event; it's a way of life. It's not for a limited time, but for our whole life."[12] Discipleship is not just for beginners, but for everyone in God's family. It is for everyone and must run through everything we do.

Once we have become a disciple of Christ, then discipleship is living as disciples or apprentices of Jesus Christ. So I define discipleship as Michael Wilkins does. Discipleship, he says, is "the ongoing process of growth as a disciple."[13] Or, it's what I would call the process of ever-increasing formation of Christ in our lives. It involves making other disciples of Christ while Jesus is discipling us. But to *make* disciples we must *be* disciples. That is the D² process in action.

What Is Discipling?

Whereas discipleship is the ongoing process of commitment and growth in Christ to become disciples, *discipling* is our part in aiding that commitment and growth in others. Remember D²?

First, we are becoming disciples, which is a life-long journey. But the second part of D² is discipling others while we are being discipled. As we make disciples, we call people to follow and imitate the growing Christ in us (not our own self in all its sinfulness). Perhaps that is why we often do not find ourselves discipling others. We are afraid.

- Afraid that we don't know enough.
- Afraid that our relationship with Christ isn't what it should be.
- Afraid to stick our noses into other people's lives since we are well aware of our own sinfulness.
- Afraid to call others to follow and imitate us because we are unsure that we are truly following Christ.

Yet Paul was not afraid to call others to follow and imitate him and, in turn, to disciple others in the same way. Please study these very bold statements that Paul made:

- "I do not write these things to make you ashamed, but to admonish you as my beloved children. For though you have countless guides in Christ, you do not have many fathers. For I became your father in Christ Jesus through the gospel. I urge you, then, be imitators of me. That is why I sent you Timothy, my beloved and faithful child in the Lord, to remind you of my ways in Christ, as I teach them everywhere in every church." (1 Cor. 4:14–17)
- "Be imitators of me, as I am of Christ." (1 Cor. 11:1)

- "Brothers, join in imitating me, and keep your eyes on those who walk according to the example you have in us." (Phil. 3:17)
- "You yourselves know how you ought to imitate us." (2 Thess. 3:7)
- "Set the believers an example in speech, in conduct, in love, in faith, in purity." (1 Tim. 4:12)
- "Show yourself in all respects to be a model of good works, and in your teaching show integrity, dignity, and sound speech that cannot be condemned, so that an opponent may be put to shame, having nothing evil to say about us." (Tit. 2:7–8)

Having considered all of those passages, I agree with Wilkins's definition of discipling as "the responsibility of disciples helping one another to grow as disciples."[14] In other words, this is our role and responsibility in helping others toward spiritual maturity. And spiritual maturity only happens through the process of *spiritual formation* in our lives.

What Is Spiritual Formation?

In discipleship and discipling we are simply joining the Holy Spirit in his work of spiritual formation: the process of being formed, conformed, and transformed into the image of Christ through the leading and guidance of the Holy Spirit. The role of the Holy Spirit is to transform us into the image of Christ. This is what many people call "spiritual growth." While discipleship is the ongoing process of becoming a disciple, and discipling is our active role in that process to help others become disciples, spiritual formation is the Holy Spirit's role. Consider spiritual formation in the way Paul shared it with the Corinthians. He told them, "I planted, Apollos watered, but God gave the growth. So neither he who plants nor he who waters is anything, but only God who gives the growth. He who plants and he who waters are one, and each will receive his wages according to his labor" (1 Cor. 3:6–8). According to this passage, one might understand seed planting as evangelism and watering as discipleship/discipling, but spiritual formation is God through his Holy Spirit causing the growth from the inside out.

Based on what I have just shared, you might be wondering, "What about evangelism? What part does it play in all of this?" Those are great questions. Evangelism is seed planting by the spreading of the Christian gospel through public preaching or personal witness. It comes from the Greek word *euangelion*, which means "good news." Evangelism is the spread of God's good news (gospel) of salvation found only through Jesus Christ, as expressed throughout the whole of Scripture.

Evangelism is the first step of opening people up to the gospel. They need to hear the word to receive it. As Paul says in Romans 10:14, "How then will they call on him in whom they have not believed? And how are they to believe in him of whom they have never heard? And how are they to hear without someone preaching?" Evangelism is our role in spreading the good news of Jesus Christ so that people can call on the name of Jesus to be saved and to become his disciples. It is a crucial step. Yet evangelism is a part of the discipleship process, not the whole of it. It is the beginning step in the overall process of discipleship. Unfortunately, we have often made evangelism the end. If we can bring people to the water, then we have done our job. But it is only the beginning. True discipleship and discipling are carried out over a lifetime, not a moment. It is important that we keep this in mind as we move forward and grow.

The answers to these questions and their subsequent definitions will now guide us through the following chapters. By these definitions, we discover that our goal is to allow the Holy Spirit to use us to help others (and ourselves) to move toward transformation into the image of Jesus. Disciples making disciples. The D^2 process. We must take an active role in this process as described to us in the Great Commission.

Chapter 4

Holy and Wholly Living

What do you love most? The answer to that question determines what someone makes his or her god. Whatever we love most is seen in where we spend most of our time, where we spend most of our resources, and whatever most of our thoughts and affections are directed toward. Since the beginning, God has wanted us to love him more than anything else. Why? Because he knew that what we love most is our god. What we make our god is what we will draw from to make life decisions. Our god becomes the lens through which we see and interact with the world.

What are you seeking in God? It is important for us to ask this question before we start considering what kind of relationship God wants to have with us. What we are seeking in God will determine what sort of relationship we will have with him. The Gospel of John records an interesting incident that should make all of us think about this question. In John 1:35–51, John the Baptist is talking with two of his disciples when he sees Jesus passing by. As he sees Jesus, John alerts his disciples, "Behold, the Lamb of God!" Intrigued by John's claim, the two disciples begin to follow Jesus. Jesus notices their pursuit and turns to them and asks, "What are you seeking?" They both respond to Jesus calling him "Rabbi," which John defines as "teacher" in the text. So we understand that at first they recognize Jesus as a rabbi.

Then the text tells us that one of the two disciples is Andrew, Peter's brother. He goes and finds Peter and tells his brother, "We have found the Messiah." John again defines the title in the text and says that "Messiah" means "Christ." This title of "Messiah" or "Christ" is given to Jesus by his early followers and indicates what they were seeking in him (an "anointed one" or king). Yet, there is one more important claim in this passage concerning Jesus.

Jesus tells Nathanael that he is a man of no deceit and that he had seen Nathanael earlier under a fig tree. Evidently, Jesus must have seen Nathanael under the fig tree in some supernatural way, because Nathanael responds by saying, "Rabbi, you are the Son of God! You are the King of Israel!" While this title "Son of God" is linked with the idea of the expected king of Israel, it also carries with it superhuman connotations, recognizing Jesus as the king above all kings, the One who would come from God.

Possible Choices

In this passage, we encounter several individuals who are seeking something. What or who they are looking for we can't be sure, but they certainly are seeking. I want to call attention to a few points in this passage. First, Jesus turns to the two disciples who are following him and asks the question, "What are you seeking?" I want to propose that Jesus continues to ask his followers that same question today. So what are *you* seeking? Second, I believe the responses of the disciples in this story give us three potential answers to that question. Before we can move on to discuss the sort of relationship God is seeking with us, we first have to consider what sort of relationship we are seeking with him. I believe these three relationship options are choices we still must choose from today. Let's explore them.

Rabbi/Prophet

The first two disciples respond to Jesus by calling him "Rabbi" (or "Teacher"). Later on, in chapter 9 of John, when the man born blind is asked who he believes Jesus to be, he responds, "He is a prophet." In another instance in Luke 24, two disciples are walking on the road to Emmaus after the death of Jesus. His identity still unknown to them, Jesus begins to travel with them and asks why they look so sad. They tell him that their sadness has to do with Jesus's death, and they describe Jesus as "a man who was a prophet mighty in deed and word before God and all the people" (Luke 24:19).

Jesus was known to many as a rabbi or prophet, roles best described as teachers or bringers of the Word of God. These are titles or descriptions most people still feel comfortable using to label Jesus. In fact, many people (from all faith walks, or lack thereof) would recognize Jesus as a good teacher. This recognition does not require too much of a commitment. One can recognize another as a good teacher or orator, even follow them for a while (perhaps gaining some notoriety from the relationship), but remain unchanged with a very low level of commitment or devotion to the teacher.

Judas had this kind of relationship with Jesus. Though he followed Jesus for some time, he was known to be focused on more worldly matters than the path of Jesus. In fact, Judas is the only one of the twelve disciples who was never recorded calling Jesus anything more than rabbi. Consider the time in Matthew 26:20–25 when Jesus predicted that one of the Twelve would betray him. The disciples were saddened by Jesus's prediction and began asking him one-by-one, "Is it I, Lord?" Jesus didn't come out and say exactly who it is. Instead, he told them it was the one who has dipped his hand in the bowl with him. That could have been any one of them, of course, and, in fact, they all did turn away and leave him at one point. Yet, in this instance, only one of them called Jesus something different. Only Judas responded to Jesus with, "Is it I, Rabbi?" To which Jesus answered, "You have said so."

Notice that the other eleven addressed Jesus as "Lord," but Judas found it sufficient to call him rabbi. I don't want to read too much into this passage, but I find it interesting that it is recorded in Scripture in this particular way. Perhaps Judas was drawn into betraying Jesus because he never saw him as anything more in his life than a good teacher. Even Muslims believe that Jesus was a good teacher.

Now, don't get me wrong here. I believe that all followers of Jesus start at this point in their relationship with him. During this rabbi/teacher time, we see Jesus as holding something of great importance to our lives that may bring something good to us. At some point, however, we have to decide whether Jesus will remain simply a good teacher to us or become something more. That brings us to our second relationship option with Jesus.

Messiah/Lord

To simplify the definitions of these titles, it is easiest to recognize "Messiah" as the "Anointed One" (king/savior). "Lord" can simply be understood as a master or ruler. If we go back to John 1 for a moment, we see that Andrew, one of the two that initially addressed Jesus as rabbi, now describes Jesus to his brother Simon in this way, "'We have found the Messiah' (which means Christ)."

Again, John defines his own use of titles so that the reader will be clear about who the early disciples believed Jesus to be.

Returning to Luke 24, we find that the two disciples who walked on the road to Emmaus with Jesus, once they realized they had been with Jesus, returned to Jerusalem to tell the disciples that they had seen him. Though they first described Jesus as a mighty prophet in verse 19, they now describe him to the disciples by saying, "The *Lord* has risen indeed, and has appeared to Simon!" (emphasis added). Did you see the movement there? They went from calling Jesus rabbi or prophet to Lord after they had seen him in his power, risen from the dead. Maybe they were simply using the titles interchangeably, but it seems to me that in their exclamation, they were making a declaration of who they believed Jesus to be.

If this is so, then perhaps moving from a rabbi or teacher relationship to a Messiah or Lord relationship requires more. At this level, people are willing to allow Jesus to be Messiah or Lord, which means they are willing to allow him to be their ruler or master of their lives because they believe he will lead them to where they want to go. This kind of master is not unlike a boss. I think we can all understand that concept. You will follow a boss as long as you think he will get you where you want to go and help you get what you want to have.

Many Christians fall into this relationship category. Just like Andrew, they have come to confess Jesus as Lord of their lives. Why? Because he can save them, and that's what it takes to be saved. After all, don't we all want to be saved and go to heaven? In order to get my "heaven ticket" punched, I need to confess Jesus as Lord and Savior of my life. At this level of relationship, you will "mostly" do what Jesus asks of you—unless it is counter to where you want to go or what you want to do. Then you will fudge on it with full assurance that you've been saved and Jesus washes away sins. In other words, "I'm still good, and he's still Lord." But is that all God expects of us? In the D² frame of spiritual growth, where we are becoming disciples in order to make disciples, isn't there something more than this half-hearted commitment to "being a disciple"? The answer to that question is in our final relationship option.

God

At some point in our relationship with our rabbi and Lord, we have to decide whether we are willing to make him our God. When God is God, that's all there is. He is the "I AM." It's not a recognition of a title or a role; it is a confession of who he is and who we are *not*. Consider Peter's response to Jesus in John 6. In the last half of this chapter, Jesus is sharing some difficult teachings about who he is. In fact, he's calling his disciples to eat his flesh and drink his blood. To a Jew, if they interpreted this literally (as some were doing), this would have been against God's law on many fronts. Therefore, when many of the disciples (you heard me, disciples) hear these words, they turn away from following Jesus and no longer walk with him.

When Jesus sees many of his disciples—his followers—turn and walk away, he looks to the Twelve and asks them, "Do you want to go away as well?" (John 6:67). What a question! I feel as if Jesus turns to us often and asks that same question. When his teachings challenge our thinking and, more importantly, our way of living, do we want turn and go our own way? It is then that I believe he looks at us and asks, "Do you want to go away as well? What were you seeking in me?" He is looking for individuals who will respond to him as Peter did, "Lord, to whom shall we go? You have the words of eternal life, and we have believed, and have come to know, that you are the Holy One of God" (John 6:68–69).

Thomas had a similar "aha" moment with Jesus in John 20. Back in chapter 11, Thomas had made the bold statement about his Lord Jesus, "Let us also go, that we may die with him" (John 11:16). However, after Jesus's death, Thomas had not yet seen his Lord and he emphatically expressed his doubts of the resurrection. "Unless I see in his hands the mark of the nails, and place my finger into the mark of the nails, and place my hand into his side," Thomas said, "I will never believe" (20:25). What a turn in faith and boldness! Yet all of us would probably admit to doubting Jesus at times in our lives in much the same way.

Eight days later (yes, this apostle doubted Jesus's resurrection for eight days) Jesus appeared among the disciples and challenged Thomas to put his fingers in his wounds and believe. When Thomas saw his Savior, his only response to Jesus was, "My *Lord* and my *God*!" Somewhere in our relationship with Jesus, we must make the same difficult confession—the hardest one of all. Not just rabbi or prophet, not just Messiah or Lord, but *God*! But that confession is more than words. I often tell people that our confession does not reflect our actions. Think of Peter. Shortly after his confession of Jesus as Lord and Christ, he also denied him. Our actions reflect our true confession. So the question remains: "What are you seeking?" Are you seeking a rabbi or prophet, a Messiah or Lord, or God? The answer to that question drastically impacts your relationship with God and his view of your love for him.

God is not satisfied with a part-time relationship. The Shema in Deuteronomy 6:4–5 states, "Hear, O Israel: The LORD our God, the LORD is one. You shall love the LORD your God with *all* your heart and with *all* your soul and with *all* your might" (emphasis added). Jesus repeated those words when he was asked what the greatest command was. He said, "The most important is, 'Hear, O Israel: The Lord our God, the Lord is one. And you shall love the Lord your God with all your heart and with all your soul and with all your mind and with all your strength.' The second is this: 'You shall love your neighbor as yourself.'" Then he told his questioners, "There is no other commandment greater than these" (Mark 12:29–31). Once God had shared with his children that he alone was God, he wanted to make sure they knew how he wanted them to love him: *holy* and *wholly*. This means that God sets us apart (makes us holy) as his children and asks that we love him not in part, but in whole—heart, soul, mind, and strength (wholly).

God desires to have a deep and intimate relationship with his children because of his great love for us. He initiates this relationship with his children through his Spirit. The Holy Spirit connects with us through our soul and spirit (our inner core) and then infiltrates all other areas of our being. God is not only asking us, "What are you seeking?" He is also turning to us and asking, "Do you love me?"

Do You Love Me?

This is the core of discipleship. We are constantly being asked by God, "Do you love me?" This was Jesus's frame of reference when he restored Peter after he had denied Jesus (John 21:15–19, 22). In this passage, Jesus looked at Peter and asked him, "Simon, son of John, do you love me more than these?" Peter responded to Jesus, "Yes, Lord; you know that I love you." Based on Peter's response, Jesus then instructed him to feed his lambs. Again, Jesus asked Peter, "Do you love me?" Once again Peter told Jesus, "You know that I love you." Jesus gave Peter a second instruction: "Tend my sheep."

One more time, Jesus asked Peter, "Do you love me?" For a moment, recognize that Jesus asked this question three times. It is interesting that Jesus asked the same question the exact number of times that Peter denied him. But this time the text tells us that

Peter was hurt and said to Jesus, "Lord, you know everything; you know that I love you." Jesus then gave Peter the same instruction, "Feed my sheep." One of the most interesting things about this passage is that after Jesus had this conversation with Peter (and then told him how he would grow old and die), he then gave Peter one final instruction, "Follow me." Now let's consider all of this a bit more closely.

Three times Jesus asks Peter, "Do you love me?" With each question, Jesus also has instructions. The instructions give Peter a way to demonstrate his love for Jesus. The instructions are also linked with Ezekiel 34 when God is rebuking the elders of his people. They have neglected their roles as shepherds and have fed themselves rather than God's children. So God says that he himself will care for his flock—that *he* will (1) seek the lost, (2) bring back the strays, (3) bind up the injured, and (4) strengthen the weak (34:16).

God told the Israelites he would do this by setting up over his people one shepherd who would come from his servant David. He said that through this one shepherd he would be with his flock and would be their God, and his shepherd would be among his people. Jesus fulfilled this role as our one good shepherd. He lived out seeking the lost, bringing back the strays, binding up the injured, and strengthening the weak. And when he was about to leave this earth, he instructed his disciples to live out his mission among his people.

The instructions he gives to Peter in John 21 simply tell him how to imitate the life that Jesus has already lived in fulfillment of Ezekiel 34. The instructions apply to us today as we seek to demonstrate our love for God. Consider his instructions in this way:

Do we love Jesus more than these (fill in the blank with your "these")? If so, then:

- **Feed my lambs and seek the lost.** Help the helpless by sharing God's love with those who do not know him. Our role is to share the gospel message with the lost and helpless.
- **Tend my sheep (bring back the strays and bind up the injured).** Tend to the hurting children of God. Our walk of faith is difficult, and we must care for each other so that Satan does not get a foothold in any believer's life. We must guard against the attacks of Satan on the family of God.
- **Feed my sheep (strengthen the weak).** Feed the hungry. Those who hunger for God's Word and his love need constant feeding. As fellow-children of God, we must be diligent with our soul-feeding so that our love and attention are constantly directed back toward Jesus. When we are hungry and are not fed with the right food, we will find anything that will provide us momentary sustenance. When we fail here, we begin to allow our brothers and sisters to become malnourished, and they will find themselves feeding on the refuse of the world.

After Jesus provides these instructions, he gives Peter a final charge: "Follow me" (21:19, 22). To follow Jesus, we must come after him, deny ourselves, take up our crosses daily, and then follow him (Matthew 10:37–39; 16:24–26; Mark 8:34–38; Luke 9:23–24). Only then can we truly follow Jesus as his disciples. Once we have accepted this relationship as disciples (the first leg of D²), we begin to grow spiritually as God has found "good soil" (Matt. 13:3–8, 18–23) that is receptive to his Word (both Jesus the Word and the written Word). God tills and prepares this good soil in us through our hearts, souls, minds, and strength so that the soil can grow and bear his good fruit.

Heart, Soul, Mind, and Strength

I could talk a lot about what exactly the heart, soul, mind, and strength of a man or woman are. A wide range of discussion offers multiple interpretations. But I want to focus on the basic understanding that God intends for us to love him with every bit of who we are. As humans, we recognize there are different aspects of our selves, and Jesus alludes to them here. What are these different aspects?

- **Heart.** The heart represents our emotions, the seat of our love and affection. The Hebrew hearers would have understood heart (*lēbhāb*) to mean seat of intellect, will, and intention (and possibly emotions and feelings). As God has a passionate love for us, he in turn desires that we passionately love him. Check out Deuteronomy, for example, to see how many times Moses reminded his people to serve God "with all their heart and soul and mind and strength" (4:29; 13:3; 26:16; 30:2, 6, 10). Or consider how often Jeremiah foretold doom for his people because of their stubborn refusal to be fully devoted to their Creator (3:17; 9:13–14; 11:8; 13:10; 16:12; 18:12; 23:17). Jesus often alluded to these scriptures and affirmed their call to total commitment (Matt. 10:28; 16:24–26), and the apostle Paul also echoed the prophet's warnings when he wrote, "Because of your hard and impenitent heart you are storing up wrath for yourself on the day of wrath when God's righteous judgment will be revealed" (Rom. 2:5). The need for us to be wholehearted in our love for God comes across clearly in both the positive and negative biblical statements about it.
- **Soul.** The soul (*nephesh*) would have meant "being or life" and would have been understood in a broader sense to

express "the whole inner self, with all the emotions, desires, and personal characteristics that make each human being unique."[1] Some believe that the pairing of heart and soul proposes "a distinction of some sort is being made between mental and emotional energy and activity."[2] For our understanding, the soul is that moral or "spiritual center" part of us that "connects with God." Since we have "no other gods," our one and only God takes up residence in that center, and we meet with him there through worship, prayer, spiritual disciplines, and other practices if, as both Moses and Jesus said, we do so "with all our souls."

• **Mind.** Our mind involves our intellect and thoughts. It is our ability to think rationally, to reason, to process information, and to arrive at conclusions. Yet our mind is more than an idea factory or a memory bank; it's also the storehouse of our attitude and emotional disposition. We are to have the mind of Christ, Paul wrote (Phil. 2:5). As he struggled with how hard it was for him to control his body, in contrast, he said, "I myself serve the law of God with my mind" (Rom. 7:25). "Do not be conformed to this world," Paul instructed his readers in Rome, "but be transformed by the renewal of your mind, that by testing you may discern what is the will of God, what is good and acceptable and perfect" (12:2). Obviously, ignorance won't win us any brownie points in Christian circles. When the assembly of the Corinthian church was being disrupted by disorderliness, Paul rebuked them and told them that they, just as he did, should both pray and sing not only "with my spirit" but also "with my mind" (1 Cor. 14:14–15). Our minds must always be focused on those things that are pleasing to the Lord.

• **Strength.** Strength or might (*mĕ'ōd*) is the physical side of each human with all its capacities and functions. It quite literally means our "very." The specific notion being used here is that of "muchness" and that Israel should love God with all of its essence and expression.[3] Some interpret "might" (the KJV's traditional word choice here) to mean our money and possessions, while others believe that self-discipline is required so that God can be loved with all one's might.[4] So our "strength" here would mean all we own as well as our behavior and how we put things into action. And we want our possessions and how we use them as well as our behavior and actions to reflect our heart (emotions), soul (moral and spiritual center), and mind (thoughts and intellect). Both Moses and Joshua admonished their people to serve God "with all your heart and with all your soul" (Deut. 10:12; 11:13; Josh. 22:5). For them, it needed to be all or nothing. New Testament church leaders echoed this call for total commitment. James told his people that mere beliefs alone were not enough; they needed to effectively combine faith and works (2:14–26), and the apostle John agreed. "Let us not love in word or talk but in deed and in truth," he wrote (1 John 3:18). "Whatever you do, in word or deed," Paul instructed his converts, "do everything in the name of the Lord Jesus, giving thanks to God the Father through him" (Col. 3:17).

With all of that in mind, we cannot compartmentalize our love and devotion to God. He (and our love for him) must encompass every aspect of our lives. Consider the visual in how we are to love God.

In the image on page 78, recognize that the inner self, the heart, of a person is the core of who they are. In this core self is a hole. That hole may be filled with anything or anyone we choose. God placed that hole there for a purpose. Ecclesiastes 3:11 says, "He has also set eternity in the human heart; yet no one can fathom what God has done from beginning to end" (NIV). God intended that hole (eternity) to be filled with him, yet we humans struggle with understanding it. So we often try to fill the hole with everything or everyone else but God. Yet that hole is never filled until God is set firmly in it. Only when he fills the hole in our hearts will we truly find fulfillment.

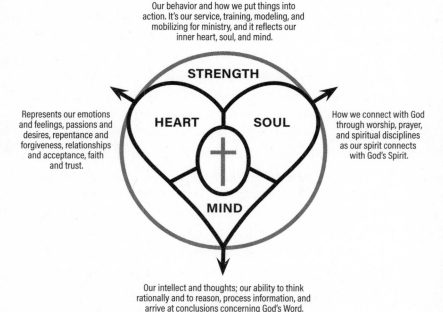

Our behavior and how we put things into action. It's our service, training, modeling, and mobilizing for ministry, and it reflects our inner heart, soul, and mind.

Represents our emotions and feelings, passions and desires, repentance and forgiveness, relationships and acceptance, faith and trust.

How we connect with God through worship, prayer, and spiritual disciplines as our spirit connects with God's Spirit.

Our intellect and thoughts; our ability to think rationally and to reason, process information, and arrive at conclusions concerning God's Word.

As you continue to look at the image, you can see that the heart (our inner self) has three aspects (yet is unified and whole). There is the heart (representing our feelings, passions, desires, and forgiveness), the soul (how we connect with God through worship, prayer, and spiritual disciplines as our spirit connects with the Spirit), and the mind (our intellect and thoughts, our ability to think rationally and to reason, to process information, and to arrive at conclusions). Those three aspects of our inner self work and function together to make us who we are. It is from our core that we act and behave, which is our strength (our possessions, behavior, and how we put things into action). We want our behavior and actions to reflect our heart (emotions), soul (moral and spiritual connection with God), and mind (thoughts and intellect).

If we fail to know this and live accordingly, we fail to know and live the very essence of Scripture and the very essence of who we are. The Israelites were commanded to place the commandments "upon their hearts." It's evident that God has always wanted his children to think on, meditate about, experience, and live out "these words" (the Shema).

Phases of Spiritual Formation

Understanding those aspects, we can discover and discern some phases of spiritual formation that are essential to our progress in D^2. As I studied this, I discovered that others were finding similar phases of spiritual formation. You can look at Willow Creek's *Reveal*, Jim Putman's *DiscipleShift*, and others to see similar phases or stages of spiritual growth. During my own studies, however, I found that the phases of spiritual growth closely mimic the phases of our physical growth. So, in my D^2 explorations, I used common phrases from developmental psychology to differentiate what I believe to be the distinguishable phases of spiritual formation—what I call a "Spiritual Formation Continuum."

Imagine the continuum as a set of stairs. Each phase of our lives moves us up those stairs toward a more intimate relationship with Christ as we continue to be transformed into his image. We must not "get stuck" on any one of those steps. Instead, we must make every effort to move steadily up them. Each stage of the continuum has identifiable markers to indicate what phase we are in. Again, we want to move from one stage of spiritual formation to the next. So in the next section, I have provided some important questions and key indicators for each phase that will assist you in discovering where you are at on the continuum.

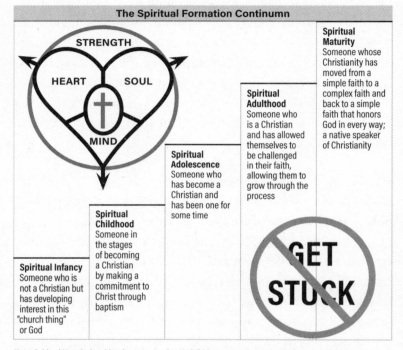

The Spiritual Formation Continumn

Spiritual Maturity
Someone whose Christianity has moved from a simple faith to a complex faith and back to a simple faith that honors God in every way; a native speaker of Christianity

Spiritual Adulthood
Someone who is a Christian and has allowed themselves to be challenged in their faith, allowing them to grow through the process

Spiritual Adolescence
Someone who has become a Christian and has been one for some time

Spiritual Childhood
Someone in the stages of becoming a Christian by making a commitment to Christ through baptism

Spiritual Infancy
Someone who is not a Christian but has developing interest in this "church thing" or God

STRENGTH
HEART   SOUL
MIND

GET STUCK

Note: Spiritual Maturity is evident in someone when their faith serves as the catalyst for how and why they think about things, provides the means and focal point for "centering" themselves, defines their interactions with others, and defines and shapes how they deal with the world.

Please remember that these indicators are dynamic and not static. We will often move up and down the stairs as we grow and encounter things in our lives. So at any moment, we may exhibit indicators from a phase above or below. This does not mean we are stuck, but it may indicate an area of needed growth. The point is that we are always pointed up toward God and not toward the world. We are moving and not standing still.

Maturity along the Spiritual Formation Continuum

Let's do a quick analysis of each state in the continuum to get a solid grasp on where we may be and where our disciple-trainees may be right now on the stairway toward spiritual maturity.

Spiritual Infancy

Someone who is not yet a Christian and has a developing interest in this "church thing" or God.

Heart
- Is heavily influenced by the world
- Lacks trust in relationships
- Struggles with feelings of acceptance ("Can I come? Do you mean me too?")
- Questions whether forgiveness is possible

Soul
- Has an inherited or passed-down faith
- Seeks God through prayer or Bible reading only when in need (Is there a God and who is this Jesus? What does Jesus mean to me?)

Mind
- Has little to no biblical knowledge
- Has little understanding of moral absolutes
- Learns one-on-one with a minister or close personal friend

Strength
- Has little to no practice of faith

Needs
- Worship: Spectator
- Develop relationships through:

- Orientation classes
- Bible classes
- Small groups (for connection purposes)
- Gender specific activities (men's breakfast, women's Bible class, others)
- Service opportunities

Spiritual Childhood

Someone in the stages of becoming a Christian by making a commitment to Christ through baptism.

Heart
- Is in beginning stage of trust in God and his people (need for relationships)
- Knows forgiveness is possible, but it is still questioned

Soul
- Understands faith is taught versus owned (for example, "I heard a brother say . . ." versus "I believe . . .")
- Makes time sporadically for personal Bible reading and prayer

Mind
- Has exposure to basic biblical principles that builds a framework (rule set) that guides thinking and development
- Learns through Sunday morning sermons

Strength
- Understands the need to serve, but self will take precedence over service

Needs
- Worship: From spectator to partaker (24/7 or 52/7)

- Begin practicing "acts of righteousness"
  - Personal study of God's Word
  - Silence, solitude, meditation
  - Prayer
  - Giving
  - Fasting
  - Others
- Deepens relationships through:
  - Bible classes
  - Small groups (for depth)
  - Gender-specific activities (men's breakfast, women's Bible class, others)
  - Service opportunities

Spiritual Adolescence

Someone who has become a Christian and has been one for some time. Unfortunately, a stage where too many disciples get stuck.

Heart
- Begins to find a place and knows what one can do in the midst of community by recognizing one's own spiritual gifts and how they can be used
- Feels forgiven and accepted in the church

Soul
- Begins to see oneself in the story of faith rather than just knowing the story of faith
- Sees growth as one moves from a faith based on external direction or motivation to one that is grounded in a unique identity found only in Christ
- Needs to move from an inherited or obligated faith to a faith built on convictions

- Makes time for personal Bible reading and prayer most days

Mind
- Connects biblical principles to practice in daily life
- Begins to ask, "What do I believe and why?" for a deeper understanding of the link between biblical principles and practice
- Learns in Bible classes and small groups

Strength
- Feels obligated to serve and share faith (though this occurs infrequently)

Needs
- Worship: From partaker to contributor
- Discover spiritual gifts through assessment and mentoring (for feedback)
- Begin involvement in ministry
- Help teach a Bible class
- Practice of "acts of righteousness" becomes a habit
  - Personal study of God's Word
  - Silence, solitude, meditation
  - Prayer
  - Giving
  - Fasting
  - Others
- Deepens relationships through:
  - Mentoring
  - Accountability group

Spiritual Adulthood

Someone who is a Christian and has allowed themselves to be challenged in their faith. Therefore, they have grown through this process.

Heart
- Tends to look beyond oneself to the care, love, and nurture of others

Soul
- Begins to enjoy daily communion with God through prayer, study, worship, and other practices (that have become reflective, thoughtful, contemplative) as a daily practice of living God's grace that informs every act, word, or thought
- Lives the process of building a liberating faith rather than a restrictive one
- Reaches the crisis of re-entrenching to a more simplistic form of faith (Spiritual Adolescence or earlier) or one that is thoughtful and discipleship oriented

Mind
- Has a foundation firm enough to discuss biblically prescribed issues while being able to differentiate prescribed from traditional practices
- Has challenges in the formation of a thoughtful simplicity (that is, the ability to reflect on complex issues, yet find the peace that comes with simplicity)

Strength
- Learns through practice as one finds oneself teaching, leading service projects, becoming a ministry leader, mentoring others, and others

Needs
- Worship: From contributor to initiator
- Initiate ministries
- Initiate worship opportunities
- Initiate a Bible class or study
- Initiate a small group
- Practice "acts of righteousness" daily and help others through mentoring
- Personal study of God's Word
  - Silence, solitude, meditation
  - Prayer
  - Giving
  - Fasting
  - Others
- Deepens relationships through:
  - Mentoring others
  - Small group
  - Accountability group
  - Service opportunities

Spiritual Maturity

Someone whose Christianity has moved from a simple faith to a complex faith and back to a simple faith that honors God in every way. A "native speaker" of Christianity.

Heart
- Desires what God desires, implying that one's emotional life has been transformed and formed
- Surrenders to Jesus as Lord and reveals this surrendering through one's actions (self-surrender is central to this stage)

- Has faith marked by a trust, confidence, and hope in God that has developed over time

Soul
- Owns faith that can be explained and shared
- Breathes personal Bible reading and prayer—it just happens!

Mind
- Has self-directed learning
- Augments knowledge and study (history, evolution of doctrine, comparative studies, and others)
- Completes deeper, more nuanced studies in Scripture and application to life

Strength
- Moves beyond believing and acting "correctly" to practicing from Christian motives
- Shares belief and knowledge in growth groups and personal mentoring
- Shares God's grace naturally and obviously in daily life (the journey is not complete, but only beginning)

Needs
- Worship: From initiator to imitator
- You cannot *not*:
  - Love Jesus
  - Love others
  - Share Jesus
  - Serve Jesus
  - Serve others
- "Acts of righteousness" are breath (one *must* breathe in God's Word, talk with him unceasingly) and *must* be shared (Jer. 20:9)

- Personal study of God's Word
- Silence, solitude, meditation
- Prayer
- Giving
- Fasting
- Others
- Deepens relationships through:
  - Ongoing mentoring relationships
  - Some relationships have moved from mentoring to apprenticeship
  - Others seek this person's counsel
  - Others join this person in what he or she is already doing (they want to imitate this person because he/she imitates Jesus)

So where are you on the continuum? As you consider each of the phases, where do you fall in the continuum of spiritual formation? Only you can answer that. It's important to regularly assess which phase you are in, and even to have others assess where they think you are. This assessment allows for a time of both introspection and discovery as you see how others view your walk with Christ. Both are helpful strategies toward continued growth so that you don't allow yourself to get stuck along the way.

Here are some possible questions you can ask as you assess yourself and others:

1. What are you doing to intentionally prepare and cultivate the soil of your heart (your emotional self) so that you may form a healthy relationship with God and others?
2. What are you doing to intentionally prepare and cultivate the soil of your soul (your spirit) so that you may be receptive to God?

3. What are you doing to intentionally prepare and cultivate the soil of your mind (thoughts, intellect, attitude) with the renewing of the mind, so that you can think and reason according to the Scriptures?

4. What are you doing to intentionally prepare and cultivate the soil of your strength (faith and love in action) so that you are prepared for works of service and evangelism to build up the family of God?

The answer to those questions will help you discover what phase you are in or what phase others say you are in. You can then begin to form a plan of how you would like to grow and move further toward spiritual maturity. Look inward and allow others to share with you what they see in you. I pray this will be a blessing and will motivate you to move forward while you encourage others to do so. That's the D² path. May God bless you on your journey.

Chapter 5

What Does a Disciple Look Like?

What does a disciple look like? Have you seen one lately? What distinguished him or her from everyone else? Often, I have people ask me to share with them evidence of someone being a disciple of Christ. At first, I found myself struggling to put it into words. I was convinced I knew what a disciple of Christ looked like, but I didn't know quite how to express it in words. Well, like anything else, it took examining God's Word to discover the description, or profile, of a disciple of Jesus Christ. And that description turned out to be a critical part of the whole D^2 process. How can we become a disciple, or make one, if we don't know what one should look like?

A Biblical Profile of a Disciple of Christ

Based on everything I studied and discovered in the preceding pages, and after looking more deeply into passages about disciples in Scripture, I found the following to be the best biblical descriptions of a disciple of Christ (one who truly follows Jesus). I hope this will provide you with motivation to grow in Christ and become more like him every day.

1. **A disciple is committed**. A disciple of Christ is someone who has devoted his or her self to the Lordship of Jesus. He or she denies self and puts Christ first in every aspect of life. This is an eternal commitment. Jesus describes this kind of commitment in the Sermon on the Mount with the famous prayer he taught his disciples to pray (Matt. 6:9–13), his warning that we cannot serve two masters (6:24), and his instruction that his people should always "seek first the kingdom" (6:33). Anyone serious about following Jesus must take up their cross daily, Christ tells us (Luke 9:23). After he washes his disciples' feet, Jesus says truly committed disciples will imitate his servant spirit (John 13:13). Those who are genuinely committed to Christ will "no longer live for themselves but for him who for their sake died and was raised" (2 Cor. 5:15).

2. **A disciple is obedient**. A disciple is committed to a life of submission to Christ. A disciple surrenders his or her life to God and continually says yes to what God asks them to be or do. Like the people in Moses's day, the Lord tests us to "know whether you love the LORD your God with all your heart and with all your soul" (Deut. 13:3). If we are Christ's disciples, we are no longer "our own" because we were "brought with a price" (1 Cor. 6:19–20). If we really belong to Jesus, this will tame our tongues, calm our tempers, purify our behavior, and improve our relationships, just as Paul tells us in Ephesians 4:22–5:5. If we truly belong to Jesus, the apostle John makes it clear that we will carefully keep all of

his commandments and won't consider this requirement a burden (1 John 5:1–5).

3. **A disciple is a lifelong learner**. A disciple of Christ is open to the leading of the Holy Spirit and is teachable. He or she is not a "know it all," but instead is growing spiritually over a lifetime. "Give instruction to a wise man, and he will be still wiser," the sage of Proverbs assures us. "Teach a righteous man, and he will increase in learning." Then he focuses on the kind of learning that matters most. "The fear of the Lord is the beginning of wisdom, and," as all true disciples of Jesus know, "the knowledge of the Holy One is insight" (Prov. 9:9–10). Jesus promised to teach his chosen Twelve how to *become* "fishers of men" (Mark 1:17). This means that a disciple (as a lifelong learner) is always in a state of becoming. Some disciples found Jesus's teaching and training hard. And John tells us that many turned away and no longer walked with him. Jesus knew why. No one could come to him unless they were drawn to him by the Father (John 6:60–66). When disciples are drawn to Jesus, they are willing to wrestle with the difficult teachings in order to be with Jesus. Like Peter, they confidently say, "Lord, to whom shall we go? You have the words of eternal life, and we have believed, and have come to know, that you are the Holy One of God" (68–69). Disciples who spend their lives learning the Lord's truths are like that.

4. **A disciple is a fruit bearer**. A disciple practices spirituality to be transformed by the Holy Spirit and to demonstrate the fruit of the Spirit in his or her life: "Love, joy, peace, patience, kindness, goodness, faithfulness, gentleness, self-control" will be the characteristics of true disciples of Jesus (Gal. 5:22–23).

5. **A disciple is devoted to prayer and practices**. A disciple spends time in daily devotion and is constantly developing his or her prayer life. How many of us are like the psalmist David, who sang that his one consuming desire was to spend time in the Lord's house, to "gaze upon the beauty of the LORD and to inquire in his temple" (Ps. 27:4)? Christ's disciples will long for the same kind of communion with the Savior. A later psalm writer poured out similar feelings: "As a deer pants for flowing streams," he sang, "so pants my soul for you, O God. My soul thirsts for God" (42:1–2). That's how we should feel about Jesus. Jesus himself modeled for us this continual desire to pray. Passages like Mark 1:35 and Luke 11:1–4 illustrate that Jesus frequently retreated for prayer.

6. **A disciple is shaped by the Word**. A disciple longs to learn and apply the Word of God to his or her life. One does this through hearing the word preached and taught, reading the Bible regularly, going to group Bible studies, memorizing Scripture, and meditating on the Scriptures. "If you abide in my word, you are truly my disciples," Jesus tells us (John 8:31). Luke praised the first converts in the little town of Berea for their diligence to study God's Word. Unlike others up the road a few miles, Luke said these disciples "received the word with all eagerness, examining the Scriptures daily" (Acts 17:11)—a good model for Jesus's disciples anywhere any time. "Let the word of Christ dwell in you richly, teaching and admonishing one another in all wisdom," is Paul's solid advice for all who follow Jesus (Col. 3:16). Paul also writes, "Do your best to present yourself to God as one approved, a worker who has no need to be ashamed, rightly handling the word of truth" (2 Tim. 2:15).

7. **A disciple is a servant**. A disciple is God's servant who actively engages in helping others in practical ways, just as those early disciples in Jerusalem took care of the widows among them (Acts 6:1–4).

8. **A disciple is a witness**. A disciple wants to be a witness for God and to share his message of salvation. A disciple intentionally presents the gospel regularly with increasing skill, thereby obeying our Lord's command that we preach the Good News to everybody everywhere, baptizing and teaching them so that they, too, can become his disciples (Matt. 28:18–20). Jesus calls us to be his witnesses, just as he commissioned his first disciples to be (Acts 1:8). Romans 1:16 tells us that the gospel that drew us to salvation is the power God will use to save others. Our job as disciples is to share it. The sacred traditions passed on from Jesus's first disciples either by spoken word or by written letters must now be communicated and kept alive by us (1 Thess. 2:4).

9. **A disciple is a cheerful giver**. A disciple honors God through his or her time, possessions, and finances. No Christian should ever be forced to give, but God loves those who do give cheerfully (2 Cor. 9:7). The first Christians were taught to plan ahead and give weekly to support worthy causes (1 Cor. 16:1-2). It's a good model for us to follow as well.

10. **A disciple is faithful**. A disciple faithfully meets and enjoys fellowship with other members of God's family (through church services, Bible studies, discipleship groups, prayer groups). In those contexts, his or her spiritual needs are met and, in turn, can make a contribution to the body of Christ. All disciples of Jesus should be like the psalmist David, who said he was glad when his comrades said to him,

"Let us go to the house of the LORD!" (Ps. 122:1). The church of Jesus gains strength when disciples show up regularly to study and worship (Acts 16:5). The Christian fellowship is like a human body, Paul writes in 1 Corinthians 12. The body of Christ is healthy and capable only when all of its members are filling their role. When one part is missing, all the parts are affected. Jesus's disciples are encouraged not to get into the habit of skipping worship, but to be faithful in gathering with fellow believers to "stir up one another to love and good works" (Heb. 10:24–25). When we gather to enjoy fellowship with other believers, Scripture assures us that we also will enjoy fellowship "with the Father and with his Son Jesus Christ" (1 John 1:3).

Expectations of Christ's Disciples

As I looked over this biblical profile of a disciple of Jesus, I began to ask myself if it points to expectations of what it means to be a part of the family of God. I kept the following question in front of me to see what God would lead me to do: *What does it mean to be a disciple of Christ?*

Every family has a set of expectations that family members observe (whether spoken or unspoken). The expectations guide how the relationships between family members work. In church families, expectations often are not discussed and are shied away from. We are afraid that in sharing them, we will run people off.

Expectations for involvement in team sports, civic and volunteer organizations, school, and other activities are well known and placed on every member of society. Yet the work of the Lord's church carries much more weight than any of those secular pursuits. I believe that the lack of impact for Christ in our nation (and perhaps the world) may be attributed to the sad fact that little to no expectations are placed on church members. As we see in the

New Testament, members of the Lord's family must be committed to ministry through their local church.

Based on all the discussions of discipleship in the preceding pages, I do not want to shy away from the fact that there are expectations for all disciples in the Lord's family. Instead, I would like each of us to understand how the family of God works and what is expected of each family member. I desire that each member of God's family be an active participant in the kingdom work that is going on in their local church. The following is my best attempt to be faithful to what Scripture outlines as "family expectations" in the Lord's church.

- **I will believe.** I believe that Jesus Christ is the Son of God. I believe that he died on a cross to set me free from sin. I believe that he rose from the grave with the promise to raise me from the grave—both physically and spiritually—to live with him for eternity in heaven. "Whoever does not believe will be condemned," Jesus warns (Mark 16:16); but he also promises, "Whoever believes in me, though he die, yet shall he live" (John 11:25). The Gospel accounts of Jesus's life and works, such as those in John, were written for this express purpose: "that you may believe that Jesus is the Christ, the Son of God, and that by believing you may have life in his name" (John 20:31). On this point, the Word of God is clear. To be saved, we must believe in Jesus (Acts 16:31; Rom. 5:1–2; 10:4, 9–11; 1 Cor. 15:3–11).

- **I will commit.** I will commit my life to Christ and become his disciple (a follower or apprentice of Jesus). I understand that part of my commitment is to repent of my past life of sin, to confess Jesus as my Lord and Savior, and to be baptized into his name and thus be added to his family. (If you have any questions about God's plan of salvation,

please don't hesitate to ask someone in your local church.
I know they will be happy to explain what they believe the
Bible teaches on the subject. Ultimately, it is your decision.)
From the first days of his ministry, Jesus taught people to
repent—to regret their sins and turn away from them. And
Jesus told his disciples to teach that same message (Luke
24:45–47). After Jesus ascended, his disciples preached
repentance just as Jesus had told them to (Acts 3:19; 17:30;
2 Pet. 3:9). Those who came to Jesus not only made a silent
commitment to him, but they also openly confessed their
faith in Jesus, knowing that he had promised to confess
their names in heaven (Matt. 10:32). Paul writes, "If you confess with your mouth that Jesus is Lord and believe in your
heart that God raised him from the dead, you will be saved"
(Rom. 10:9–13). And over and over in the New Testament,
we see that people who came to faith in Jesus wanted to be
baptized. They wanted its cleansing power (Acts 2:38; 1 Pet.
3:21). They wanted to connect with Jesus's death and resurrection by reenacting them in water (Rom. 6:1–7; Col. 2:12).
The disciples who were helping others become disciples
assured them, "As many of you as were baptized into Christ
have put on Christ" (Gal. 3:27).

• **I will worship.** I understand that being a member of the
Lord's church means that I will meet regularly with other
members of God's family to worship him with all my heart,
soul, mind, and strength in Spirit and in truth. The earliest
Christians were warned not to get out of the holy habit of
meeting with their fellow disciples (Heb. 10:25). And believers who were of Jewish heritage surely were not surprised
at this. The Psalms are filled with declarations to worship:
"Worship the LORD in the splendor of holiness" (29:2). God's
people have been counseled in every age to "come into his

presence with singing" (100:2). Christians today are no different. Jesus himself requires this: "You shall worship the Lord your God and him only shall you serve" (Matt. 4:10). The hour has come "when the true worshipers will worship the Father in spirit and truth, for the Father is seeking such people to worship him" (John 4:23). All Christians should hear the inspired call, "Let us offer to God acceptable worship, with reverence and awe" (Heb. 12:28). Worshiping is something all Christ's disciples do.

- **I will grow.** I understand that part of my commitment to Christ is to grow spiritually as his disciple. I know that growth takes place not only individually, but also with other brothers and sisters in Christ. So I will work to foster my spiritual growth through Bible studies, a growth group, spiritual disciplines, and any other means that may help me grow and be transformed into the image of Christ. Every disciple of Jesus starts off as a baby. We're on a milk diet, "unskilled in the world of righteousness" (Heb. 5:13); but, as the very next verse says, we need to mature so that we can eat "solid food" for our souls. "Like newborn infants, long for the pure spiritual milk, that by it you may grow up into salvation," the apostle Peter wrote (1 Pet. 2:2). Even the apostle Paul realized that he had to grow up in Christ (Phil. 3:12–15). All of us do. So the Scriptures encourage us to "grow in the grace and knowledge of our Lord and Savior Jesus Christ" (2 Pet. 3:18).

- **I will serve.** Like Christ, I understand that I did not become a disciple of Christ to be served, but to serve others and to give my life for the sake of Christ. I recognize that I am a part of the body of Christ and have been given gifts by the Holy Spirit for the purpose of building up the body of Christ and those in need. I understand that to serve is to sacrifice. To sacrifice is to give up what may be best for me for the good of others and for the glory of God. Therefore, I will work each day to be a living sacrifice to God. The first description of disciples in the new church of Acts tells how many of them sold their property to aid others among them who were in need (Acts 2:45). It remains a perfect description of a true Christian. In addition, Paul compares Christians to farmers. If we skimp on the seeds we sow, our crop will be scant. But he assures fellow disciples that "Whoever sows bountifully will also reap bountifully" (2 Cor. 9:6–15). All of us in Christ have some gift, talent, or special possession that could become a blessing to our fellow disciples. If we want to be like Jesus, we'll use whatever we have to serve others (1 Pet. 4:8–11).

- **I will share.** I commit to living out the Great Commission by going out and sharing my faith with those who do not know the Lord. I want to share the love and grace of God that have been freely given to me through Christ so that others may know and share in those blessings with me. As he prepared to leave this earth, Jesus instructed his first disciples to tell everybody everywhere about the blessings they could find in him (Matt. 28:18–20; Mark 16:15–16). They energetically and courageously became his witnesses, even when telling the truth about Jesus got them flogged and imprisoned, as we see in Acts 4:18–20 and 5:27–32, 40–42. If I am a real disciple of Jesus, I too will be willing to pay whatever it costs to tell others about him.

- **I will give.** I understand that God loves a cheerful, generous spirit. I know that in giving to my church family, I am giving to the work of God by giving my time, talents, and treasures. I know that all I have is his and that giving back to him is just a small portion of what he has given me. I understand that through giving, I am helping fund and promote ministries and missions that support the expansion of God's kingdom and help those in need. When I give, I will never do it to draw favorable attention to myself. Jesus warned us about that (Matt. 6:1–4). Most of us are like those first disciples of Jesus; we have to grow in the grace of giving (2 Cor. 8:1–15). What and how much we give is always up to us, but we learn over time that the blessings God gives to his people tend to grow as our giving increases, just as the Scriptures promise (2 Cor. 9:6–15).

- **I will seek unity.** I understand that others will know I am a Christian by how I love my brothers and sisters in Christ. So I will seek to bring unity rather than division in my church family. I commit to seeking out my brother or sister when I know I have wronged them or I know they have sinned against me. I will model the reconciliation of God to those around me by loving others as Christ has loved me (John 13:34–35; 15:12). As a disciple of Jesus, I will do my best to live at peace with other disciples so that our unity will attract others to him (John 17:20–23). I will make sure that I cause unity, not division, among the believers in my community, just as the Bible tells me to (1 Cor. 1:10). I will forgive any disciple who wrongs me, just as Jesus forgives me (Col. 3:12–14).

- **I will pray.** I know that God listens to me and longs for me to talk with him. So I will commit to be a person of prayer. I will regularly kneel before my God on behalf of others and myself and will seek to grow in my relationship with God through continual conversations with him. Sometimes I will pray the prayer Jesus gave us to pray (Matt. 6:5–15; Luke 11:1–4), but whether in such a set ritual or in everyday life, I will follow Jesus's instructions to "always" pray (Luke 18:1). When I'm down or discouraged or distressed, I will pray (Luke 21:36). As Scripture instructs, I will "be constant in prayer" (Rom. 12:12), "praying at all times in the Spirit" (Eph. 6:18; Col. 4:2). In good times and bad, I will "pray without ceasing" (1 Thess. 5:17).

- **I will honor and respect.** I understand and respect and will commit to honoring the direction that God and my spiritual leaders have laid out before me. I understand that as a member of God's family, I put myself under the oversight of leaders of the church, and I will work to honor them as they commit to shepherd me in my walk with Christ (Acts 20:28). They are my valued "overseers," according to God's Word (Phil. 1:1; 1 Tim. 3:1–7; Titus 1:5–9). They shepherd me under the Chief Shepherd, Jesus, so I will do everything I can to make their spiritual task as pleasant as possible, just as Peter instructed (1 Pet. 5:1–4).

I hope these expectations demonstrate to you a desire to honor God and his will and purpose for our lives as his disciples. When we live them out, then they should demonstrate the deep love we have for God and his people and how we want to intentionally live out his mission in our lives. I hope you will allow God to use your God-given gifts in faithful, humble service to him as you commit to fulfill these expectations for the glory of God.

How Do We Know If We Are Growing Spiritually?

All of the characteristics just described are biblical, and most of us know they should be the qualities and expectations of a disciple of Christ. However, you might be asking yourself at this point, "How do I really know if I'm growing spiritually?" We all know that we can fake it. We can put on a good show by attending church, by serving once in a while, and maybe even by teaching a class or going on a mission trip. But all the while, we may be unchanged inside. We may be going through the motions without being fully devoted to God. So how do we really know if we are allowing the Spirit of God to grow us and transform us? What is the evidence of spiritual growth and transformation?

In the parable of the soils, Jesus refers to spiritual growth as bearing fruit. Those who not only hear the word and receive or understand it—those who not only process the Scriptures in head and heart—but also put it into action are moving from knowledge and understanding to wisdom (motivating and activating our hands) and are demonstrating spiritual maturity. This is exhibited through an individual's actions and is the fruit they bear. Jesus says, "As for what was sown on good soil, this is the one who hears the word and understands it. He indeed bears fruit and yields, in one case a hundredfold, in another sixty, and in another thirty" (Matt. 13:23). This metaphor was used as far back as Solomon's day when it was written in Proverbs 11:30, "The fruit of the righteous is a tree of life, and whoever captures souls is wise."

Remember, disciples are different from those who simply hear the word of Jesus and have some understanding of it. They need more than concepts to understand; they need actions to live out. When they begin to live a disciple's life, their thoughts, behaviors, attitudes, and actions reflect the one they follow. This is the fruit they bear and by which they are known. Jesus pursues this idea when he says, "Every healthy tree bears good fruit, but the diseased tree bears bad fruit. A healthy tree cannot bear bad fruit, nor can a diseased tree bear good fruit. Every tree that does not bear good fruit is cut down and thrown into the fire. *Thus you will recognize them by their fruits*" (Matt. 7:17–20—emphasis added). Jesus then goes on to say in the next verse, "Not everyone who says to me, 'Lord, Lord,' will enter the kingdom of heaven, but the one who *does* the will of my Father who is in heaven" (emphasis added).

When we are in step with and fulfilling the will of our Father in heaven, we bear fruit in keeping with his character (not fruit in keeping with our sinful nature). But the only way we can stay in step with the will of God is to stay in step with the Spirit who is leading us toward him. The struggle comes with the warring factions of our flesh (our sinful nature) and the Spirit. Paul spoke plainly of his flesh/Spirit struggle in Romans 7 as he tries to fulfill God's Word while his sinful nature is still so strong within him:

> We know that the law is spiritual, but I am of the flesh, sold under sin. For I do not understand my own actions. For I do not do what I want, but I do the very thing I hate. Now if I do what I do not want, I agree with the law, that it is good. So now it is no longer I who do it, but sin that dwells within me. For I know that nothing good dwells in me, that is, in my flesh. For I have the desire to do what is right, but not the ability to carry it out. For I do not do the good I want, but the evil I do not want is what I keep on doing. Now if I do what I do not want, it is no longer I who do it, but sin that dwells within me. So I find it to be a law that when I want to do right, evil lies close at hand. For I delight in the law of God, in my inner being, but I see in my members another law waging war against the law of my mind and making me captive to the law of sin that dwells in my members. Wretched man that I am! Who will deliver me from this body of death? (Rom. 7:14–24)

All of us struggle with this. But there is hope. Paul discovered that even though this war is raging within us, "There is therefore now no condemnation for those who are in Christ Jesus. For the law of the Spirit of life has set you free in Christ Jesus from the law of sin and death" (Rom. 8:1–2). By sending Jesus, God condemned the sin of the flesh so that what the law required might be fulfilled in us. What a wonderful God we serve! Those who are devoted to God walk not by the flesh, but according to the Spirit. As Paul said, "Those who live according to the flesh set their minds on the things of the flesh, but those who live according to the Spirit set their minds on the things of the Spirit" (Rom. 8:5).

But how do we keep from setting our minds on the things of the flesh and instead set our minds on the things of the Spirit? This battle within reminds me of the Native American Tale of Two Wolves:

> One day, a tribal elder is teaching his grandson about life. "A fight is going on inside me," he says to the boy. "It is a terrible fight and it is between two dogs. One is evil—he is anger, envy, sorrow, regret, greed, arrogance, self-pity, guilt, resentment, inferiority, lies, false pride, superiority, and ego." He then continued, "The other is good—he is joy, peace, love, hope, serenity, humility, kindness, benevolence, empathy, generosity, truth, compassion, and faith. The same fight is going on inside you—and inside every other person, too." The grandson thought about it for a moment and then asked his grandfather, "Which dog will win?" The elder simply replied, "The one you feed."

The moral of the story is clear. If we continue to feed our flesh, then the flesh will win. But if we choose to be fed by the Spirit of God, then by the Spirit we are led and live our lives accordingly. So, just as I have been saying, when we rest our knowledge and understanding on the things of the Spirit, then he grows and matures us to walk by the Spirit and to demonstrate this by how we live our lives through the wisdom he has given us (by the fruit we bear). Paul went on to tell the Romans:

> You, however, are not in the flesh but in the Spirit, if in fact the Spirit of God dwells in you. Anyone who does not have the Spirit of Christ does not belong to him. But if Christ is in you, although the body is dead because of sin, the Spirit is life because of righteousness. If the Spirit of him who raised Jesus from the dead dwells in you, he who raised Christ Jesus from the dead will also give life to your mortal bodies through his Spirit who dwells in you. (Rom. 8:9–11)

Kenneth Boa notes, "The Christian life is the life of Christ in us; without a moment-by-moment reliance on the Holy Spirit, this level of living is impossible."[1] Why? Because the Holy Spirit is the Spirit of the Father and Jesus Christ (Rom. 8:9) and, as he dwells within us, he works to conform us to the image of Christ from the inside out. Without this, it is impossible for us to live as Christ and to grow spiritually. Boa continues: "Spiritual maturity is directly proportional to Christ-centeredness. To be more preoccupied with the subjective benefits of the faith than with the person and pleasure of Christ is a mark of immaturity. The Spirit bears witness to and glorifies Jesus Christ; spiritual experiences, whether personal or corporate, should center on Christ and not ourselves."[2]

When we walk in step with the Spirit, we walk in step with God. He grows and matures us into Christlikeness. When this happens, our lives bear witness, and those who witness our lives know we belong to Jesus beyond a shadow of doubt. The problem is that too many want to wear the name of Jesus without allowing his Spirit to transform their lives. They want the benefits without the commitment. A. W. Tozer once said that "the average professed Christian lives a life so worldly and careless that it is difficult to distinguish him from the unconverted man."[3] When people look at you and how you live your life, would they think you are in step with the Spirit or in step with the world?

The Fruit of the Spirit

In Galatians 5, Paul describes the way we know if we are in step with the Spirit. Paul tells his readers that if they walk by the Spirit, then they will not gratify the flesh (the sinful nature). Why is this important? The desires of the flesh are in opposition to the desires of the Spirit of God. Because they are so opposed to each other, we usually are able to distinguish between the things of man and the things of God. The works or fruits of the flesh are very evident: sexual immorality, impurity, sensuality, idolatry, sorcery, enmity, strife, jealousy, fits of anger, rivalries, dissensions, divisions, envy, drunkenness, orgies, and things like these (Gal. 5:19–21). In the same way, if we are in step with the Spirit of Christ, our fruit is evident to all.

"The fruit of the Spirit is love, joy, peace, patience, kindness, goodness, faithfulness, gentleness, self-control; against such things there is no law. And those who belong to Christ Jesus have crucified the flesh with its passions and desires. *If we live by the Spirit, let us also keep in step with the Spirit*" (Gal. 5:22–25—emphasis added). Simply put, this is how we know we are growing spiritually. If we are growing in the fruit of the Spirit in increasing measure, then we are growing spiritually. The fruit of the Spirit is the very essence of God's character and, therefore, should be the essence of ours. If we are

- loving in increasing measure,
- exhibiting joy in increasing measure,
- at peace in increasing measure,
- patient in increasing measure,
- kind to others in increasing measure,
- good to others in increasing measure,

- faithful to God and others in increasing measure,
- gentle to others in increasing measure, and
- exhibiting self-control in increasing measure, then . . .

we are growing spiritually!

The Fruit of the Spirit

Let's take a quick look at each manifestation of the fruit of the Spirit so we can know what we are looking for.

- **Love**—Love appears first because it is the greatest quality (1 Cor. 13:1–13; 2 Pet. 1:5–7). Why? Because it is this quality that most clearly reflects God's character, for "God is love" (1 John 4:16). The word used for "love" in Scripture is much more than a feeling or emotion. Instead, it looks deep into the heart and expresses an attitude of admiration and devotion to God and others. Love, according to God, is not dependent on whether one deserves it but is instead given freely without the expectation of receiving the same love in return. Love that is a fruit of the Spirit is free and unconditional.
- **Joy**—Joy comes in close behind love. For as we display joy because of God's saving grace, we show that our affections are directed toward God's will and his purpose. Jesus wants his joy to be in his disciples (John 15:11). He alone can make our joy complete (John 16:24). The joy of the Spirit comes only from above (Rom. 15:13; 1 Pet. 1:8; Jude 24). Joy is not the synonym of happiness. It is delight that is not dependent on whether something good or bad has happened. As a matter of fact, joy is delight given by the Holy Spirit, and it often shows up during the hardest times. It happens when you focus on God's purposes for your life rather than the circumstances you find yourself in (Jas. 1:2–4).

- **Peace**—Peace is what happens when sinners recognize that God has saved them from his wrath so that they are no longer his enemies. This allows us to approach God in confidence and freedom (Rom. 5:1–2; Heb. 4:16). Peace does not mean there is no turmoil in our lives, but that serenity is present even in the midst of chaos. It is a sense of contentment in knowing that God is in control (Phil. 4:6–7, 11–13). Simply put: peace is not the absence of conflict, but the presence of God.

- **Patience**—Patience demonstrates that we are content with following God's plan and that we know his timetable is better than ours. We display patience when we have abandoned our own ideas about how the world should work. Words also connected with this fruit are perseverance, long-suffering, forbearance, lenience, and steadfastness. It is the ability to suffer the mistreatment of others toward us without actively seeking revenge or paying back, the ability to "bear with one another in love" (Eph. 4:2). Paul says that God demonstrated this kind of patience when God accepted him in spite of his sins (1 Tim. 1:15–16). We see the full force of patience when we are able to demonstrate it during harsh times of "tribulation" (Rom. 12:12). Real love is patient, Paul writes (1 Cor. 13:4).

- **Kindness**—Kindness means that we show others goodness, generosity, and sympathy as God does toward us (Rom. 2:4). Kindness is demonstrated when one looks for ways to adapt to meet the needs of others. It means that one does not hold malice toward another but instead is kind to them in the same way that Jesus shows us kindness when we don't deserve it.

- **Goodness**—Goodness is when we work for the benefit of others and not for ourselves (Gal. 6:10). All that is good is of God. Therefore, goodness reflects the character of God. When you see goodness in someone, you see God. And the goodness in you longs to witness goodness in others. That means you are willing to confront and rebuke the "badness" in others so that God's goodness in them may surface (as Jesus did with the money changers in the temple and with the Pharisees and Sadducees).

• **Faithfulness**—Faithfulness means consistently doing what one says one will do just as God does. A faithful person is a person of integrity. They are someone you look to as an example because they are truly devoted to Christ and others. Our sinful nature always wants to be in control, but faithfulness that is led by the Holy Spirit is demonstrated when one seeks the good of others for the glory of God.

• **Gentleness**—Gentleness is not weakness or the absence of power. Rather, gentleness chooses to defer to others. It forgives others, corrects with kindness, encourages and strengthens others, and lives in peacefulness. It is a quality that Jesus attributes to himself in Matthew 11:29.

• **Self-control**—Self-control is the ability given by the Holy Spirit to help disciples of Christ resist the power of the flesh (Gal. 5:17). As Paul taught us in Romans 7 and 8, our flesh and the Spirit are continually at odds with one another because our sinful nature always wants to be in charge. (You know: the warring dogs inside us.) Self-control is "letting go" of these fleshly desires and choosing instead to allow the Spirit to be in control of our lives. It is refocusing the power, authority, and control of our lives back to its proper place.

Growing in each of these characteristics of Jesus Christ is a sign that the Spirit is at work within us. It demonstrates that the Spirit is transforming every aspect of who we are so that we will reflect the character and attitude of Christ. It's staying in step with the Spirit. When we do that, we produce all nine qualities of God that we just listed. When we allow the Holy Spirit to lead us instead of being led by our selfish desires, God's Spirit produces this fruit in and through us, and it is evident to all those around us. With this in mind, do you actively depend on the Spirit's guidance so that you don't get wrapped up in yourself, or do you allow your desire to "be your own god" control you? Remember, since the beginning, it has always been a matter of choice.

Staying in step with the Spirit is participating in God's divine nature. Peter tells us in 2 Peter 1:3–10 that God's power has given us everything we need to live a life of godliness, of holiness. How? Well, he has given us knowledge about himself through his great promises. These promises have been fulfilled in Jesus Christ and have given us the ability to partake in God's divine nature. The divine nature allows us to escape from the world and from our sinful desires so that we can truly live godly lives through the blood of Christ and the power of God's Spirit working in and through us.

According to Peter, knowing this should compel us to spiritual growth by supplementing our "faith with virtue, and virtue with knowledge, and knowledge with self-control, and self-control with steadfastness, and steadfastness with godliness, and godliness with brotherly affection, and brotherly affection with love" (2 Pet. 1:5–7). So we can see that our love is perfected (the end result) in Christ through a spiritual growth process that must be intentional on our part. Peter goes on to say,

> If these qualities are yours and are increasing, they
> keep you from being ineffective or unfruitful in the
> knowledge of our Lord Jesus Christ. For whoever lacks
> these qualities is so nearsighted that he is blind, having

> forgotten that he was cleansed from his former sins.
> Therefore, brothers, be all the more diligent to confirm
> your calling and election, for if you practice these quali-
> ties you will never fall. (2 Pet. 1:8–10)

Peter is simply listing the fruit of the Spirit in this passage while using slightly different terminology. He tells us that practicing these qualities will make us "fruit bearers" and will keep us from falling—not because of anything that we have done (not by works), but instead because we are walking with the Spirit through the grace of God.

When we are doing so, we will be able to see more clearly. We will keep ourselves from having "nose vision" instead of "20/20 spiritual vision." What is nose vision, you ask? Nose vision is the inability to see beyond the end of our noses. It is the nearsight-edness that Peter is speaking of. All we can see is ourselves, and everything else beyond is blurry. 20/20 spiritual vision allows us to see beyond ourselves. It allows us to see with the eyes of Jesus through the power of the Spirit at work within us. When we have that sort of vision, we will be kept from being ineffective or unfruitful. We will confirm our calling by living in the divine power of God.

So the question is, do you see the fruit of the Spirit in increas-ing measure in your life? Do you have 20/20 spiritual vision? If you do, you are growing spiritually. Remember, the fruit of the Spirit is evident. The fruit of the Spirit is an outward sign of an inward transformation. When the fruit of the Spirit is evident in increas-ing measure in your life, then you will look like a disciple of Jesus Christ. Know this: we will never live out the Spirit's fruit perfectly, but we will be in step with the One who can.

Developing a Plan for Spiritual Growth

We have learned a great deal about what it means to be a true disciple of Christ. We now know that it is all encompassing and requires vigilance on our part to continue to grow more and more into the image of Christ. To continue in our growth in Christ, we must make plans toward that end. Think about it this way: everything important in your life has required planning. Everyone's personality is a little different, so they plan in different ways, but they plan nonetheless. You could pick anything big that happens in a person's life: weddings, graduations, going to college, or moving. Each of these requires a great deal of planning toward accomplishing a particular goal. Let's choose going to college as an example.

A student who wants to succeed in a particular field to gain employment in that area will spend a great deal of time looking at the different colleges that offer degrees in that field. The student will begin to see which colleges offer the best options (that is, financial aid, location, well-known and respected teachers in the field, student-to-teacher ratios, length of program, grading scales, job placement after graduation percentages, and so on). Once the student has narrowed down the field of choices, he or she then might visit the campuses of the universities, meet with faculty, sit in classes, and visit the dorms (or, if you were like me, go check out the cafeteria)—all this to simply choose the college the student believes will help them achieve their vocational goals in life.

Why would we not spend as much time planning our growth in the most important aspect of our lives—our relationship with Christ?

Jesus taught his disciples the principle of planning when he discussed with them the need to count the cost of discipleship. In Luke 14:25–33, Jesus turns to the crowds of people following him and tells them what following him truly costs. First, he tells them that it could cost your most precious relationships. He uses strong language when he says that if anyone truly wants to become his disciple, then they must love their family less than they love him. In other words, Jesus comes first and will not play second fiddle. In fact, he tells us we must love him more than we love ourselves.

Second, he tells them that one must bear their own cross before becoming his disciple (as he did in Luke 9). In fact, Jesus states that you *cannot* be his disciple unless you bear your own cross. The idea of crucifixion is a shocking metaphor for discipleship, but a powerful one. Jesus is saying that a disciple of his must deny self (or die to self-will), take up their own cross (embrace God's will, no matter how much it will cost personally), and *then* follow him. Jesus is telling them to let go of self-determination and replace it with obedience to and dependence on him.

Finally, Jesus calls his followers to count the cost of being his disciples by using two parabolic statements and questions. His two questions are: 1) "Which of you, desiring to build a tower, does not first sit down and count the cost, whether he has enough to complete it?" 2) "Or what king, going out to encounter another king in war, will not sit down first and deliberate whether he is able with ten thousand to meet him who comes against him with twenty thousand?" (Luke 14:25–33). Jesus expected that his listeners would be thinking, "Of course you would count the cost." He expects that same answer when we're determining whether to be his disciple or not. If you say yes to discipleship, then you have to give up everything for him.

Jesus not only prompts his disciples to count the cost of following him, but he also tells them to plan for it. The moment we commit our lives to Christ, we have joined him in a lifelong journey toward being transformed into his image. We are journeying with Jesus through his Spirit toward Christlikeness from the point of our acceptance and commitment to him until the day of our death or his return. If we believe this to be true, then we must not take the trip without making plans for the journey. This journey requires us to examine ourselves and to consider our walk with him.

Consider the following passages:

Psalm 26:2–3—"Prove me, O LORD, and try me; test my heart and my mind. For your steadfast love is before my eyes, and I walk in your faithfulness."

Psalm 139:23–24—"Search me, O God, and know my heart! Try me and know my thoughts! And see if there be any grievous way in me, and lead me in the way everlasting!"

Lamentations 3:40—"Let us test and examine our ways, and return to the LORD!"

Haggai 1:5—"Thus says the LORD of hosts: Consider your ways."

2 Corinthians 13:5—"Examine yourselves, to see whether you are in the faith. Test yourselves. Or do you not realize this about yourselves, that Jesus Christ is in you?—unless indeed you fail to meet the test!"

Galatians 6:4—"Let each one test his own work, and then his reason to boast will be in himself alone and not in his neighbor."

Ephesians 5:15—"Look carefully then how you walk, not as unwise but as wise."

Each of those passages and others like them attest to the need for us to continually examine our walk with Christ. Why? In order that we can know if we are walking in his way or not. This self-examination should motivate us to continually assess our current place on the map of discipleship so that we can make plans for continued growth.

Solomon understood not only planning one's course but relying on God as the guide. Meditate on the following passages (especially those portions that have been highlighted) from Proverbs:

3:5–6—"Trust in the LORD with all your heart, and do not lean on your own understanding. In all your ways acknowledge him, and he will make straight your paths."

16:1–3—"The plans of the heart belong to man, but the answer of the tongue is from the LORD. All the ways of a man are pure in his own eyes, but the LORD weighs the spirit. Commit your work to the LORD, and your plans will be established."

16:9— "The heart of man plans his way, but the LORD establishes his steps."

19:21— "Many are the plans in the mind of a man, but it is the purpose of the LORD that will stand."

It is evident from these passages that God wants us to make plans for our lives that are consistent with and in accordance with his will for our lives. He wants us to move through life with him. So if we truly want to be his disciples, we must make plans in our lives that lead us down the path toward him. This will compel us to trust in him as our God and guide, knowing that he knows best and has a plan to lead us closer and closer to him—a plan that will stand.

This is the same mindset Jesus had when he told his disciples not to worry about the needs of this life. Why not worry? Our Father, who loves us, will provide them. This is not to say that we shouldn't work and make plans in this life. We recognize that our goal is closeness to God. That goal directs all our steps and plans as we seek him in every aspect of our lives. Therefore, we do not become lazy, but instead work harder to honor him in this life and the next, just as we desire to express our love and devotion to him. Instead of worrying, our plans in life should be to seek first the kingdom of God and his righteousness in every moment of our lives (Matt. 6:2–33). God will be faithful to those who are faithful to him. What a wonderful God we love and serve!

Design Elements of a Plan for Spiritual Growth

The purpose of a plan for spiritual growth is to deliberately map our path for continued growth in Jesus. The plan can help us discover what steps we need to take to grow. Here are the customary elements of a plan for spiritual growth that could be incorporated into your own individual plan. These have been focused on for centuries and are vital elements to building our relationship with the Lord. Remember, however, that this plan is yours and will have unique elements that help you grow that may not be what others need or use. So use these as a foundation to develop your own plan, choosing those elements that you know will help you grow the most.

There are three elements I encourage everyone to have when making their own plan for spiritual growth. I didn't come up with these; God did. I am simply highlighting what God has already laid out. I call them the "Greatest Things." In Scripture, we learn what Jesus knew to be the greatest commands and the Great Commission. Simply put, the Greatest Things are (1) love God, (2) love others, and (3) go and make disciples. Following the Greatest Things allows us to create a plan for spiritual growth that honors God in the greatest ways. Let's look at these elements in more detail.

Love God

To grow in intimacy with God, we must make time to be with him regularly. Why? Because this journey is about a relationship with him. Any relationship requires time with that person to understand them and to grow in our love for them. I wonder what would have happened if when I was dating my wife and about to propose to her, I had said, "You know, I think we have something here. I believe I love you. So would you like to put a ring on this thing? Before you give me your answer, though, I need to tell you how I see this thing going. I want to spend time with you, but only when it fits into my schedule. So I'll commit to spending time with you for one hour a week and perhaps one other time, if my schedule allows for it. Maybe we can go on some weekend or even week-long trips together, but the rest of the time is mine. How's all that sound to you?" What do you think she would have said to me? "Sure, honey. As long as I can be with you. I'll give you everything and expect little in return." Ha! I know exactly what she would have said, but I'm not sure it is appropriate for me to share it here.

The point is that loving God requires a relational commitment to him. We can't expect that God would desire anything less than what we would give our spouses. In fact, he wants more! We must make sure that our relationship with God is the most important relationship we have. To keep our relationship with God thriving and growing, we must spend time with him to learn about who he is. This time will develop that intimacy that we long to have with him and that he has always longed to have with us. Here are some elements that might aid us in this area of growth:

1. **Study and meditate on God's Word.** Take time to be in God's Word every day. Find a reading plan that is right for you. Through God's Word, we get to know him as he reveals himself to us through the pages of Scripture. Not only do we learn about God, but also God speaks to us through the words and the stories. Study and meditation are a conversation with God.

2. **Prayer.** Prayer is talking to God. It's a conversation. There's no need for big words and long prayers. Just be yourself and talk with him as you would talk with the person you love the most on this earth. Thank him every day. Pray for others. Pray for his guidance. Pray for your concerns and those of others. Pray with your eyes closed or open, while sitting or standing, kneeling or lying on your bed, driving in your car, taking a shower, any place and any time. Make prayer a part of every moment of your life. Remember, pray without ceasing.

3. **Practice spiritual disciplines.** We all have a uniqueness that God created in us. Therefore, all of us will discover certain spiritual disciplines that will help us connect to God personally in a way that may be different from others. That's why it is important to discover the spiritual disciplines that help you unite with Christ. For some the discipline may be journaling, for some it may be worship through music or even art, and for others it may come through practicing hospitality. Find what your spiritual disciplines are by deliberately discovering them. It will take some trial and error, but if you seek God with all your heart and soul, you will find him. The question is, what can you do with your time to draw closer to God?

4. **Join a Bible study or prayer group.** God saw in the beginning that it was not good for man to be alone. In his great wisdom, God knew that we needed others, and so he created us to live in community. Relationships with others help us grow, but they are also messy. Often, that's why we avoid them. But we need other disciples to encourage and challenge us in our faith. We must learn from others and pray with them. This gives us an opportunity to connect with God in new ways as we encounter God through the eyes, ears, and hearts of others. While God created us uniquely, he also created all of us in his image. That means that in each person, we see a different aspect of God. As we meet with each other, we allow others to see the traits of God in us, and we see the qualities of God found only in them.

Love Others

I'm going to spend a little more time on this element because I believe our society has created an illusion that we can encounter God alone and just have a "personal relationship with God" without needing others. As mentioned earlier, though, God created us to live in community. He did not intend for us to walk this journey alone, but instead with the help of other disciples. Our growth in Christ does not happen outside of relationship: relationship with God and relationship with others. Consider those times when you experienced the greatest spiritual growth. Often, we associate those moments of growth with the people who helped us through them.

We remember that when Jesus was asked what the most important commandment was, he answered, "The most important is, 'Hear, O Israel: The Lord our God, the Lord is one. And you shall love the Lord your God with all your heart and with all your soul and with all your mind and with all your strength'" (Mark 12:29–30). We spent much of Chapter Four discussing the meaning of this and how it impacts our understanding of God and our growth as his disciples. However, Jesus wasn't finished when he had quoted the Shema (Deut. 6:4–5). He went on to explain to the question-asking scribe that the second greatest commandment is indelibly tied to the first. Jesus said, "The second is this: 'You shall love your neighbor as yourself.' There is no other commandment greater than these" (Mark 12:31).

Jesus understood firsthand that our love for God must be expressed in how we love others. As Greg Ogden says, "Essentially, Jesus is saying that these two commandments are inseparable and therefore must be treated as one. He could not imagine loving God without loving your neighbor; the natural outflow of our love for God will be our growing capacity to love our neighbor."[1]

The commandment that Jesus quotes here is found in Leviticus 19:17–18, "You shall not hate your brother in your heart, but you shall reason frankly with your neighbor, lest you incur sin because of him. You shall not take vengeance or bear a grudge against the sons of your own people, but you shall love your neighbor as yourself: I am the LORD." Here, we see that God was continuing to share with his people how to be holy before him, a holy God, so that he could dwell among them. His desire was to be with his children and walk among them.

This is demonstrated later in Leviticus after the laws had been set forth. God let his people know that if they loved, honored, and obeyed him, then he would bless them. The text says in Leviticus 26:11–13, "I will make my dwelling among you, and my soul shall not abhor you. And I will walk among you and will be your God, and you shall be my people. I am the LORD your God, who brought you out of the land of Egypt, that you should not be their slaves. And I have broken the bars of your yoke and made you walk erect." This beautiful imagery shows God's love for his children and his desire to be with them always. But for this to happen, his people had to live holy lives, set apart from the rest of the world and the cultures that surrounded them. One of the ways they would live holy before a holy God was in how they treated each other. They were not to hate or bear grudges against their brothers and sisters in the Israelite community but were instead to love their neighbors as themselves. Why? Because he is God (*Yahweh*). As God demonstrates love toward us, our natural response should be to love others. But the addition here is that we must love others as we love ourselves. What does that mean?

We live in a society where loving self is taught and encouraged. Many people find themselves dealing with a low concept of themselves, so our counselors, teachers, and leaders are telling us that we need to love ourselves, and they emphasize the building up of our view of ourselves. In fact, many of the goals involved in the humanities (psychology, sociology, counseling, and others) are centered on helping individuals grow in the following areas:

- **Self-esteem**—the reflection of a person's overall emotional evaluation of his or her own worth.
- **Self-efficacy**—the extent or strength of one's belief in one's own ability to complete tasks and reach goals.
- **Self-actualization**—the motive to realize one's full potential. Self-actualization can be seen as similar to words and concepts such as self-discovery, self-reflection, self-realization, and self-exploration.
- **Self-awareness**—the capacity for introspection and the ability to recognize oneself as an individual separate from the environment and other individuals.
- **Self-concept**—the collection of beliefs about oneself that includes elements such as academic performance, gender roles and sexuality, and racial identity, and similar words or concepts that include self-construction, self-identity, self-perspective, or self-structure. Generally, self-concept embodies the answer to "Who am I?"

The common belief is that if a person has high self-esteem, self-efficacy, self-actualization, self-awareness, and self-concept, then they will be happy individuals, live fulfilled lives, and contribute positively to society. This concept also creeps into our church families. One can find Christian publications promoting these concepts of building ourselves up in order to live successful Christian lives (or so that you can be the best you, become a better you, and live your best life now). With these concepts in mind, we can easily translate Jesus's second great commandment into, "You must love yourself well in order to love others." Ogden picks up on this and says:

> In our age, when we think low self-esteem is the root of all of humankind's problems, we have stressed loving ourselves as the means to loving our neighbor. Common therapeutic wisdom backs us up here, telling us that we can't love others if we do not love ourselves. I suppose there is some truth to that, but this can and often does lead us to emphasize the "as yourself" part more than love for our neighbor.[2]

Are you picking up on the problem with these concepts? The root of the problem is an overinflated approach to and view of the self. Jesus, quoting from Leviticus 19:18, tells us that we are to love others as we love ourselves. He didn't say we need to love ourselves to love others. Truth be told, we have no problem loving ourselves. Some may quibble with me and say that we know that individuals struggle with low self-worth and, therefore, not everyone loves themselves. To which I would respond, you are correct (kind of). Why do I say that? Low view of self comes from a skewed view of self that a broken world has taught us. Yet even with a low view of self, we still love ourselves enough to seek happiness, fulfillment, and so on.

This low view of self typically stems from what we have been taught is the ideal of human happiness, fulfillment, worth, and the like. Most of those teachings are rooted in a human-centered mindset. Yet it is exactly this view of self-love that we need to move away from, from *self* to *God and others*. We are to love others and care for their worth, happiness, survival, and souls as much as we love and care for our own. This self-love (our natural tendency to make ourselves god in place of God himself) should be redirected toward God and others. As Brooks notes, "The statement 'as yourself' does not justify the self-love advocated by modern psychology as necessary for a healthy self-image. It merely acknowledges that human beings do love themselves—far too much in fact—and that God deserves as much—actually far more."[3] Jesus is teaching us that in the second commandment, God is simply addressing humans as they are—sinners who love themselves—and that love should be turned from self to God and others.[4]

With these thoughts in mind, consider the following revisions to the earlier concepts of self-esteem, self-efficacy, self-actualization, self-awareness, and self-concept.

What if we shifted our mindset from self-esteem to *God-esteem* and defined it as the reflection of a person's overall emotional evaluation of his or her own worth based on how God values them? In this view of self, we would understand that God loved us so much that he gave his only Son to save us (John 3:16). We would come to realize that we are more valuable to God than anything else in all creation (Matt. 6:26, 30). We are worth so much to him that he knows how many hairs are on our heads, or the lack thereof for some of us (Matt. 10:30).

What if we moved from self-efficacy to *God-efficacy* and defined it as the extent or strength of one's belief in God to grant them the ability to complete tasks and to reach goals in their life based on his will and purpose for their lives? With this mindset, perhaps we would begin to commit our work and goals to God, knowing that he will establish them (Prov. 16:3). We would continue to make plans in our hearts, but we would be confident that God establishes our steps (Prov. 16:9). We would make our plans, but we would realize that God's purposes stand (Prov. 19:21). We might also remember that God gives us the gifts and abilities we need to accomplish tasks and reach goals (1 Cor. 12:1–12; Eph. 4:7, 11–16). God-efficacy helps us recognize that it is God who works in us to accomplish tasks and to reach goals for his good pleasure, not our own (Phil. 2:13).

What if we turned self-actualization into *God-actualization* and understood it as the motive to realize one's full potential as God has purposed in one's life? God knows the plans he has for each of us and the abilities he has given us to accomplish those plans (that is, our potential)—plans to give us hope and a future. If we seek God to find our potential, then God promises that we will discover it (Jer. 29:11–13). Why? Because our potential is found in God alone. God-actualization helps us trust in God and realize that he will guide us toward reaching our fullest potential that he created in each of us (Prov. 3:5–6).

What if we moved from focusing on self-awareness to *God-awareness* and defined it as the capacity for introspection and the ability to recognize oneself as created in the image of God and unique from the environment and other individuals, yet indelibly linked to God and others by design? God-awareness teaches us that we are created in the image of God and are a unique reflection of him (Gen. 1:26–28). It informs us that no one has ever seen God, but when we love one another, we see and know God as he reveals himself to us through one another (as images of God) and perfects his love in us (1 John 4:12).

Finally, what if we changed our understanding of self-concept to *God-concept* and defined it as the embodiment of the answer to "Who am I in God?" God-concept teaches us that we are, in God, new creations; the old has gone and the new has come (2 Cor. 5:17). We are a royal priesthood, holy, and God's possession (1 Pet. 2:9). We are God's workmanship created for good works (Eph. 2:10). God-concept also teaches us that we are the righteousness of God (2 Cor. 5:21); children of God (John 1:12; Gal. 3:26); and the temple of God and his Holy Spirit (1 Cor. 3:16; 6:19).

When our view of self is seen with these God-concepts rather than the previous self-oriented ones, then we will love people as God loves us. And that is exactly the type of love we are instructed to love our neighbors with. In fact, in John 13:34–35, Jesus goes a step farther with loving others. He says to his disciples, "A new commandment I give to you, that you love one another: just as I have loved you, you also are to love one another. By this all people will know that you are my disciples, if you have love for one another." Not only are we to love our neighbor as ourselves, but we also are to love them in the way that Christ loves us.

If we move our love from self to God and others, then our love will progressively become more Christ-like. This is the "new commandment." This Christ-like love will look like nothing else in the world. The new standard of love is Jesus's love, which he demonstrated in washing his disciples' feet in John 13:12–17. The foot washing pointed to Jesus's imminent death (13:6–10), even though the disciples didn't fully understand it at the time. Just a few days later, the disciples would begin to appreciate this new standard of love.

It is interesting to point out that Jesus *first* commanded his disciples to love in this way, and *then* others would come to know this love by how they demonstrated it to one another. This command is not unlike the "love your neighbor as yourself" concept we saw in Leviticus 19:17–18. Those verses instructed the Israelites to love their own brothers and sisters. Just a few verses later, however, in 19:33–34, this love was extended to the strangers who join them: "When a stranger sojourns with you in your land, you shall not do him wrong. You shall treat the stranger who sojourns with you as the native among you, and you shall love him as yourself, for you were strangers in the land of Egypt: I am the LORD your God."

Note that God calls the Israelites to love the stranger as themselves—the same way they are to love their brothers and sisters. The reason? Because they also had been strangers in Egypt in their slavery. This is essentially what Jesus is telling his disciples: "When I die for you to take away your sin, I will free you from the yoke of the slavery of sin. So, when you share that same sort of self-sacrificial love with one another and others, you will also help bring them from slavery to freedom as they come to know me through your love (*my love*)." Why? Because God is love. Read this passage out loud:

> Beloved, let us love one another, for love is from God, and whoever loves has been born of God and knows God. Anyone who does not love does not know God, because God is love. . . . Beloved, if God so loved us, we also ought to love one another. No one has ever seen God; if we love one another, God abides in us and his love is perfected in us. (1 John 4:7–8, 11–12)

This Christ-like love would propel the disciples toward continued spiritual growth as they attempt to love others as Christ had demonstrated his love to them.

This "love of others" infiltrates every aspect of the New Testament. Why? As D. A. Carson points out, "The more we recognize the depth of our own sin, the more we recognize the love of the Saviour; the more we appreciate the love of the Saviour, the higher his standard appears; the higher his standard appears, the more we recognize in our selfishness, our innate self-centredness, the depth of our own sin."[5] As the disciples learned this love and began to live it, they could not help but write about it as the Spirit of God moved them. Time and time again, the New Testament attests to God's love and how we are to share it with one another and others.

How can we demonstrate that same sort of love to one another and to those in the world? By that same love, all will know we are his disciples—when we love one another. With all this in mind, here are some strategies to aid us in loving others as a part of our plan for spiritual growth:

- **Get a spiritual guide or mentor.** The concept of life coaches and counselors are widespread in our society. Why? Because even a secular culture recognizes the need for others to help us grow in different areas of our life. A spiritual guide or mentor is someone you believe will help you grow in your relationship with God. This person is someone who you know will not allow you to settle for the status quo in your relationship with God, but instead will be willing to help you recognize your blind spots, challenge your thinking, and rebuke you when you are wrong. This person is not the one you would consult to have them tell you what you want to hear, but to tell you what you need to know. This is one of the essential elements in developing and maintaining true discipleship.

- **Attend church services and gatherings regularly.** The Bible encourages us to not give up meeting together regularly (Heb. 10:24–25). Meeting together with other disciples is fundamental to our spiritual growth. When we gather together, we learn together and have opportunities to share our lives with other disciples. God speaks to us in this way. So this is essential to our spiritual growth. God uses other disciples to help us with life's struggles or to give us encouragement when we need it most. God speaks and ministers to us through other disciples. Often, our worship services do not foster that type of relationship. You must not limit yourself to Sunday worship. Instead, take the opportunity to join others in Bible classes and other church gatherings that will foster spiritual growth.

- **Be part of a small group.** Small groups are an important context in which we can "carry one another's burdens" and challenge each other toward spiritual growth. Sadly, many kinds of smaller meeting groups are called "small groups" these days, but not all of these groups will have a positive impact on us spiritually. What we want to do is become a part of a small group with purpose. The small group we choose to become a part of should provide growth in (1) individual spiritual maturity, (2) relationships and connections with the body of Christ, and in (3) bringing others to Christ and into the body of Christ. The small group we join should help us experience changed lives. This sort of small group can be a powerful resource in your faith journey and can offer fellowship, prayer, study in God's Word, service projects, outreach opportunities, and mutual support and encouragement in your quest for spiritual growth.

• **Serve others.** We often have no problem receiving God's gift of grace. Sadly, though, we tend to struggle with extending it to others. The sign of a true disciple (of spiritual maturity) is evidence of moving from receiving grace to giving it. Paul tells Titus to show himself as a model of good works in every aspect of life (Titus 2:7–8). Why? Is this just another checklist item for disciples to do in obedience? Is it a means to bring us salvation? Not at all. Serving others is simply a sign that the Holy Spirit dwells in you and has taken hold of your heart. It is evidence that you want to extend the same love and grace to others that Jesus has already extended to you. Many opportunities exist to serve people both inside and outside the church. If you want to connect with others, then go and serve with them.

• **Become involved in a ministry group.** Churches offer many different ministry opportunities. Pray and ask God where he can use you. Ministry groups will help you get connected with other disciples who are seeking to honor God with their lives. Sometimes it takes a little time and can be frustrating. Yet you should commit to a group and seek to discover where God can use you. In doing so, he will connect you with people who will help you grow as a disciple.

- **Become involved in missions.** Missions are another way not only to serve God, but also to serve others by meeting their physical, spiritual, and emotional needs. It takes us out of our comfort zone and into a world God wants us to reach. During those opportunities, you are connecting with God, with those serving on the trip with you, and with those you are serving. If you feel like your walk with God has grown stale, go on a mission trip.

Go and Make Disciples

Jeremiah once wrote, "If I say, 'I will not mention him, or speak any more in his name,' there is in my heart as it were a burning fire shut up in my bones, and I am weary with holding it in, and I cannot" (20:9). Is the Word of God burning in our hearts? When the Word of God is in our hearts, we're like Jeremiah. We cannot help sharing the gospel message with others. Christ's disciples do not keep the gift of God to themselves. They share the life-giving message as often as possible.

The Great Commission calls us to be actively going and making disciples. When we do so, we grow as disciples ourselves. It is a natural by-product of discipling. The D² process is at work. The more we intentionally go out and disciple others, the more we grow as disciples. But do we in the church truly have a burden for the lost today? Do we recognize the importance of sharing the good news of Jesus with others, or are we content to be saved and let others fend for themselves?

These questions remind me of the Old Testament story found in 2 Kings 7. The Israelites were in a time of severe famine in Samaria because the Syrian army was besieging the land. God sent word through Elisha the prophet that he would break the famine and feed his people. Four lepers found themselves outside the city beside the gate. In the deep hunger and pain, they began to say, "Why are we sitting here until we die? If we say, 'Let us enter the city,' the famine is in the city, and we shall die there. And if we sit here, we die also. So now come, let us go over to the camp of the Syrians. If they spare our lives we shall live, and if they kill us we shall but die" (3–4).

So the four lepers decided to head over to the camp of the enemy to see if they would have mercy on them. Instead, what they found was *no one*. The Syrians had deserted their camp, because God had caused them to hear the sound of horses and chariots, and they believed that a great army was coming to take them. In a panic, they chose to escape, and they left everything behind: tents, horses, donkeys, food, treasure, and more. They left everything and fled for their lives.

When the lepers entered the camp, they saw all of this and immediately started to eat and drink what was left behind. They discovered all the treasures that were abandoned and began to take some of the silver, gold, and clothing to go and hide it away for themselves. They did this not once, but twice. It was then that they began to be convicted and said to each other, "We are not doing right. This day is a day of good news. If we are silent and wait until the morning light, punishment will overtake us. Now therefore come; let us go and tell the king's household" (9).

In light of the Great Commission, I believe that we are often like those lepers. We find ourselves besieged by an enemy, lost and dying from hunger. We are unclean and unworthy to be with others. Yet we discover that God has delivered us from our enemy's hands, and he has provided us with the spoils of the victory, without any work on our part. We have received a bountiful gift from him in place of the punishment we deserve. The gift cost us nothing, yet it cost him everything. Then we begin to feed ourselves to the full on the spoils and go hide the treasure for ourselves with no regard for others who are lost and spiritually starving to death.

Perhaps this is an image of the church today. Maybe this is why the church in many contexts is declining rather than growing. Could it be that we are satisfied with keeping the gift to ourselves? If that is the case, then we all have a choice to make. We can keep the treasure to ourselves, dig a hole, and bury it, or we can come to the same realization that the four lepers did. A disciple must come to the same conclusion and say, "We are not doing right. This day is a day of good news. God has saved us from our enemy. He has given us a gift we do not deserve in place of the punishment we do deserve. We cannot keep this to ourselves!"

As disciples we carry on the mission of Christ because we are constantly reminded of this treasure we have received and the duty we have to share it with others. We do it not out of obligation, but out of great joy in being able to represent Christ to others. The gospel is not only spoken, but (more importantly) lived. We represent Jesus in what we say and do, in whatever circumstance we find ourselves in. An illustration of this is my friend Santa. No joke! He looks like the image of Santa you have in your head at this very moment—so much so that he plays the role of Santa every year for many, many children. And he's not one of those Santa characters who only plays the role during Christmas; he looks the part all year long.

One day, he and his wife were walking down the street, running errands. As they walked, he noticed a mother and child up ahead. The child was looking intently at him and began jumping up and down and screaming "Santa, Santa!" to his mom as he continued to stare at my friend. As the two parties drew near, the mom looked at my friend with embarrassment. But my friend simply knelt down and talked with the child as a Santa should. He handed the boy one of his Santa cards that he keeps in his pocket (yeah, he has them printed). When he shared this experience with me later, he said, "You always have to be prepared to represent the suit, whether you are wearing it or not." Why? Because, you look the part. When we are disciples of Jesus, we should look the part and must always be prepared to represent "the suit," the image of Christ. But this "suit" is not so much how we look on the outside as it is who we are on the inside, who owns our hearts, and how that is expressed through our words and actions.

Another example of this is the movie *The Santa Clause*. Tim Allen's character, Scott Calvin, is thrust into the part of becoming Santa when the old Santa is accidentally killed and Scott follows the instructions on a card in the Santa suit. The card ends up being the Santa Clause, with an "e," which reads:

> In putting on this suit and entering the sleigh, the wearer waives any and all rights to any previous identity, real or implied, and fully accepts the duties and responsibilities of Santa Claus in perpetuity until such time that wearer becomes unable to do so by either accident or design.

In a similar way, we are disciples of Christ when we "clothe ourselves" with (put on the suit of) his character. As Paul tells us in Colossians, we put off our old self (our old suit), with its former behavior, and put on the new self (our new suit), which transforms us into the image of Christ (3:9–10, 12–17). We look like him and smell like him (the aroma of Christ—2 Cor. 2:15–17). We waive our right to any previous identity and fully accept the duties and responsibilities of a disciple. Therefore, we choose to put on love, which is the core characteristic and identity of Christ, and we share that love wherever we go. Sharing the gospel of Jesus is more lived than spoken. When people see the love of Christ lived in and through us, they are drawn to Christ in us, and God opens the opportunity for us to share our testimony of faith with them.

When my Santa friend shared his story with me, he said, "One of the remarkable things, for me, when kids recognize me as Santa, is how excited they become. Sometimes, they literally jump up and down. Almost always they get a big smile on their faces. Even my wife gets joy from just watching it happen. It is a wonderful gift to me to be able to walk into a room and get a room full of smiles in return. Wouldn't it be great if each of us had that effect on others as disciples of Christ?"

It would be great if when we tell people we are Christians, they would have a good feeling inside rather than looking for the nearest exit. What we have to offer is so much greater than gifts from Santa. Yet people often want to run away when they see Christians coming because they feel we will pass judgement on them rather than present them with the true gift of Jesus: *freedom*. We hold a great treasure in these jars of clay (2 Cor. 4:6–7). It is imperative that we share our faith and allow the light of the knowledge of the glory of God to shine through us.

In Chapter 7, I will provide some more specific ways to plan for sharing your faith. However, I believe that it is important to pause here for an important first step toward sharing our faith: prayer. Pray for the lost and ask God to send them your way. But be careful! Once you pray this prayer, it will be answered, and you will need to do your part once it is. Praying for our unsaved family and friends is the best way to begin reaching them for Christ. Here are some specific things to pray:

- For God to draw them to himself (John 6:44)
- That they would seek to know God (Deut. 4:29)
- For them to believe the Scriptures (Rom. 10:17)

- That Satan would be prevented from blinding them to the truth (2 Cor. 4:4)
- For the Holy Spirit to work in them (John 16:8, 13)
- That they would believe in Christ as Savior (John 5:24)
- That they would turn from sin (Acts 3:19)
- That they would confess Christ as Lord (Rom. 10:9, 10)
- That they would become disciples of Jesus through baptism (Matt. 28:19–20; Acts 2:38)
- That they would take root and grow in Christ (Col. 2:6–7)

Now that we have determined that we need a plan and have described the three essential elements needed for spiritual growth, we can move forward to actually create a blueprint for discipleship. The next chapter will delve deeper into how we can design a blueprint that is both deliberate and purposeful. Without a plan, we will often revert to simply thinking about becoming a disciple without ever actually becoming one. So let's do some planning and designing.

Chapter 7

Discipleship Blueprint

Discipling Christians involves propelling Christians into the world to risk their lives for the sake of others. The world should be our focus, and we should gauge success of those who are going out to take on the world by the disciples they are making. That's the genuine D^2 dynamic at work. Disciple-making takes place multiple times every week in multiple locations by a force of men and women sharing, showing, and teaching the word of Christ and together serving a world in need of Christ. The indwelling Spirit directs and empowers discipleship and spiritual formation, but we are called to assist each other in becoming like Jesus Christ.

Part of the vision for discipleship is to "present everyone mature in Christ" before God by studying, teaching, and discipling others through God's Word. Spiritual maturity, passion, and commitment to Christ are marked by an ever-increasing desire to follow Christ wherever he leads, and they are developed through the identification and use of gifts provided by the Holy Spirit to serve others.

The apostle Peter uses the metaphor of babies growing up to describe the maturing process for disciples of Jesus. "Like newborn infants," he says, we should "long for the pure spiritual milk, that by it you may grow up to salvation" (1 Peter 2:2). The apostle Paul employs the same metaphor as he admonishes some of his converts in Corinth for failing to mature in Christ. He scolds that he had to feed them milk instead of solid food (1 Cor. 3:1–4). Does that describe any of us? The writer of Hebrews uses the same milk and solid food metaphor (5:12), and Paul expands it in the Ephesians 4:11–16 passage we looked at earlier where he describes in detail what God provides to help us grow in Christ, emphasizing the importance of "building up the body of Christ, until we all attain to the unity of the faith and of the knowledge of the Son of God, to mature manhood, to the measure of the stature of the fullness of Christ, so that we may no longer be children" (12–14).

As we contemplate our own development as followers of our Lord Jesus, I want to encourage each of us to be intentional in our desire to grow by providing a potential blueprint for discipleship that might lead us all toward spiritual maturity. The following is a coordinated and (prayerfully) Spirit-led effort toward developing a plan for spiritual growth (see pages 157–71) to ensure that your efforts contribute in some way to the broader D² mission for discipleship: making devoted followers of Jesus Christ who passionately lead others to him.

A Plan for Discipleship

The following is a plan for discipleship, as well as some specific information on each item. Many people in the world today claim to believe or follow Jesus. But "believing in" or "following" Jesus is not always the same thing as being a true disciple of Jesus. In fact, following Jesus by today's terms can be equated with following someone on Twitter. Just because you follow someone, doesn't mean you are trying to become like him or her. I believe that in order to truly be a disciple of Christ, we must be intentional with the "how."

Therefore, we must be intentional with our own discipleship efforts and in helping each other grow toward Christlikeness. Not only is the plan intentional, but it is also a daily plan. As Jesus told his disciples, "If anyone would come after me, let him deny himself and take up his cross *daily* and follow me" (Luke 9:23—emphasis added). I encourage you to follow Jesus every day by using what I call "The Seven *E* Words" as a guide.

The Seven *E* Words

In Scripture, the number seven represents completeness or perfection. I believe that if you consistently practice the Seven *E* Words, then you will progressively grow to be more and more like Christ. So, to grow as a disciple of Christ, I encourage you to do the following.

Expand Your Knowledge of God through Reading Scripture

I encourage you to read God's Word daily and to read all the way through it each year (or at least every two years). Intentionally being in God's Word is a vital part of growing as a disciple of Christ. I have created a reading plan that I call the *Not on Bread Alone Menu*. I refer to it as a menu because I believe that the intake of God's Word is as important (if not more important) than the intake of physical food. In the same way that a well-balanced diet of physical food can cause growth, so also a full and well-balanced diet of God's Word can cause exponential spiritual growth. An unbalanced diet of God's Word can cause stagnancy and ultimately spiritual death if we go too long without solid food. As Jesus quotes from Deuteronomy 8:3, "It is written, 'Man shall not live by bread alone, but by every word that comes from the mouth of God'" (Matt. 4:4). Jesus knew that the Word of God is nourishment for his children.

Deuteronomy 30:14 says, "The word is very near you; it is in your mouth and in your heart so you may obey it" (NIV). God's Word is the spiritual food we eat to grow and become more like Christ. We all have deeply ingrained frameworks for how we perceive life and how we live it. These perceptions shape our understanding of God and, unfortunately, are many times influenced by secular worldviews and philosophies. This includes how we approach and understand Scripture.

I want to reshape your perception of God's Word in a way that is contrary to secular thought, yet is rooted in God's intent, purpose, and will for our lives. Too often, we approach God's Word the same way we approach schoolwork. With this view of the Word of God, we sadly see the Bible as simply something to gain information from. But we must see Scripture as more than *informational*; it also needs to be *formational*. The problem is that we too often see the Bible as a textbook rather than a love letter. Let me explain: When we take a class, we are required to have specific textbooks to learn more about the subject we are taking. We usually don't know the authors, nor do we care much about them, but we assume they know what they are talking about (after all, they wrote a textbook), so we should learn from them. We are assigned to read it, to take it in, and to share any knowledge we have gained through it on a test or in a paper.

When we approach a textbook, we typically look for the italicized or bold-print parts because they are key points of the text that we expect to be asked about on the test. We read the book, perhaps underline it, and get ready to regurgitate all that we have learned. Once that section of the textbook is complete, we simply move on to the next section and refer back to the former only if necessary. After we have completed the course, we use the textbook only for reference—if we ever refer to it again. It only has pertinence in our life if the subject comes up and we have a need. Otherwise, it simply gathers dust (but perhaps we intend to read through it again someday). Many times, we don't even keep the textbook. Instead, we return it so that we can gain financial credit for the next textbook we need to purchase.

While Scripture contains a vast amount of information that is important for our Christian walk, if we want to grow as true disciples, we cannot treat Scripture as a textbook full only of information. This is where a transition to viewing Scripture as a love letter helps us understand Scripture as something deeper and more formational in our lives.

When we are in a dating relationship with someone, we often receive love letters, notes, emails, and messages from that person because we cannot be physically near them all the time. That person sends love to us through the written word in order to share a portion of his or her life and feelings. When we read these written words of love, we take them into our hearts. They become part of who we are in the relationship with that person. We long to read the words over and over and feel that love and desire toward us from that person. We think on those words even when they are not readily available, and we often know at least portions (if not all) of them by heart because we have placed them in our hearts.

We must begin to see God's Word like this—not as words on a page, but as words in our hearts. As the Word dwells in us, it begins to shape us from the inside out. We need to allow Scripture to read us as much as we read it. But if it does not take up residence in our hearts, then it is simply information in our heads that may be accessed and used only occasionally.

When the Word (the Bible) is not in our mouths and in our hearts, the Word (Jesus) is not in our mouths and in our hearts. When we are biblically illiterate, we are illiterate when it comes to God, Jesus, and the Spirit. It is important to note that we don't worship Scripture; we worship Jesus. However, we come to know Jesus through God's Word. I must caution you here though: consuming God's Word will only increase your appetite for growth in your heart, soul, mind, and strength (Deut. 6:4–5).

Extend Your Understanding of God through Prayer

I believe that committed times of daily prayer are vital to our spiritual formation and discipleship. Mark 1:35 tells us, "Very early in the morning, while it was still dark, Jesus got up, left the house and went off to a solitary place, where he prayed" (NIV). Why? The better question should be, "Why wouldn't he?" It's the same question we should be asking ourselves. Why wouldn't we spend more time with the Father in prayer? Prayer is an essential aspect of being a disciple of Christ.

How often have you entered into a Bible study and heard someone say, "Let's say a quick prayer and get started"? As if an obligatory passing glance at God is enough. This statement declares, "God, thank you for attending _our_ study. _We_ have several things to go over and discuss that _we_ are working on. If you have anything to share, just chime in whenever you feel the need." Really? Are we saying that the Lord of the universe, who created our inmost being in our mother's wombs, only gets a passing glance and maybe an opportunity to share if he wants to pipe up?

Prayer is about relationship. It is about entering into the life of the one you are praying to and allowing God to enter yours. As Henri Nouwen says: "Praying is no easy matter. It demands a relationship in which you allow someone other than yourself to enter into the very center of your person, to see there what you would rather leave in darkness, and to touch there what you would rather leave untouched. Why would you really want to do that?"[1] Nouwen goes on to say that this is dangerous and often causes us to enter into a defense mode. Unfortunately, this is often our posture toward prayer: defensive. "I'll do it, but only if I can ask for things. Not if I have to tell him my darkest secrets." It's then that we make excuses for why we don't pray:

- I don't have the time.
- I don't know how.
- It doesn't really do anything for me.
- How do we know he's really listening and answering?

It's time to stop making excuses and simply talk to our Father. What do I mean by that? Brennan Manning tells a story about a three-year-old who is given a box of crayons and a coloring book by her father. The child then takes the gifts and begins to color everything coming to her imagination. The father is periodically presented with the masterpieces for approval. Upon inspection, the father discovers that the child has colored the sun black, the sky green, and the grass purple. She has added lines and rings and squiggles all through her landscape.

So what is the father's response to his child's art? Well, he does what any good father would do and praises his daughter for her beautiful renderings. Actually, he is in awe of her creativity and boldness. He puts his daughter's art up in his office and tells his staff how proud he is. Perhaps he even makes references to her early ability as an artist with Van Gogh-like tendencies. But Manning's point is that in a father's eyes, a child cannot do a bad drawing. Likewise, we cannot do a bad prayer before our Father in heaven. As Manning says,

> A father is delighted when his little one, leaving off her toys and friends, runs to him and climbs into his arms. As he holds his little one close to him, he cares little whether the child is looking around, her attention flitting from one thing to another, or just settling down to sleep. Essentially the child is choosing to be with her father, confident of the love, the care, the security that is hers in those arms.[2]

Our prayers are just like that. We leave our adult toy boxes and other worldly distractions in order to go and be with our Father—to rest in his arms and loving hands. We may be fidgety and our thoughts may dart here and there (we might even fall asleep in the night), but we are making a conscious decision to be with God. We are choosing to give ourselves over to him and receive his love and attentiveness. We are allowing ourselves to enjoy him and he us. As Manning says, "It is very childlike prayer. It is prayer that opens us out to all the delight of the kingdom."[3] God is looking for us to simply talk to him as a child, without being distracted by the world, but instead resting in his love and knowing with all our hearts that we love him. Just like this simple note my daughter, Rylie, gave me when she was little: "Dad, I love you. You are the best. Love, Rylie."

Jesus spent time with his Father in prayer to remain connected with him in relationship and to seek the Father's guidance (since he was here to do his Father's will). In Luke's narrative, prayer occurs at every major point in Jesus's life:

- At his baptism (3:21)
- At his selection of the Twelve (6:12)
- At Peter's confession (9:18)
- At his transfiguration (9:28–29)

- In his teaching the Lord's Prayer (11:1–4)
- In teaching on prayer (18:1–14)
- Before Peter's denial (22:32)
- Before his crucifixion (22:39–46)

Jesus did not want to take one step without his Father. Why would we? Albert Lemmons addresses our prayerlessness by saying:

> I am sure the devil is pleased since his *modus operandi* is to keep you from praying. He will concede to any belief and will grant what the Bible has to say about the kingdom, God's grace, even praise and worship; however, if he can keep you off your knees, you are no threat to him! It is when you become fervent in spirit and in agonizing prayer that he becomes concerned. The devil will do anything in his power to keep you from praying.[4]

Lemmons goes on to say that prayerless Christians have hindered the work of God for too long. Prayerless Christians will always make religion a cold theory, void of God's power. Without prayer, our sermons have no power. Where we find fervent prayer, we find great faith, but where prayer is minimized, so is our faith. This is a tragedy! Lemmons continues, "For one to say he/she believes in God but does not pray is a paradox, a tragedy. For one to believe in God but not pray is a contradiction, a delusion. The extent of one's prayer life may very well be the barometer of faith."[5]

Therefore, I encourage you—I implore you—to engage in a devoted time of prayer each day. My hope is that this time of prayer will expand over time, but first I encourage you to commit to spending time with God in prayer at least once a day. In asking for this commitment, I recognize that it is important to understand what prayer really is:

- **Relationship**—relating to God one-on-one for intimacy

- **Reliance**—relying on God for everything
- **Recognition**—recognizing God's presence and sovereignty in your life
- **Remembrance**—remembering who God is, what he does, and what he wants
- **Rest**—resting in him as the One who is in control and looks out for your best interest

Express Your Knowledge of God through Memorization of Scripture

Why is Scripture memorization one of the Seven *E* Words? Simply put, there is no greater way to get to know God and his ways than through his Word. Dallas Willard once said that

> Bible memorization is absolutely fundamental to spiritual formation. If I had to choose between all the disciplines of the spiritual life, I would choose Bible memorization, because it is a fundamental way of filling our mind with what it needs. This book of the law shall not depart out of your mouth. That's where you need it! How does it get in your mouth? Memorization.[6]

I believe that memorization is vital to discipleship because God's Word planted in our hearts

- Helps us come to know who God is and what he asks of us
- Provides us with ways to overcome sin
- Helps us overcome Satan
- Helps us communicate God's gospel message to those who do not believe
- Is his way of communicating to us

As prayer is our way to talk with God, study is his way of talking to us. For those reasons, I challenge individuals to memorize some portion of Scripture each week.

Explore Deeper Meanings of God's Word through Group Bible Study

Consistent group Bible studies establish smaller communities of accountability where our understanding of how Scripture affects our daily walk and our place in God's story can flourish. These different groups consist of Bible study groups, small groups, and discipleship groups.

Start by participating in some sort of a Bible study (whether at your local church or with a group you pull together). I believe that Bible study with other believers is an important part of our spiritual formation and discipleship. So begin regularly taking part in a Sunday morning Bible class or a weekly Bible study to explore God's Word with other brothers and sisters in Christ so that mutual growth can take place. With any Bible study, I have three goals in mind:

1. **Transformation.** My desire is that through the study of God's Word with other fellow-disciples, hearts will be spiritually transformed and lives changed. I do not study simply to gain information. Instead, I study for transformation, so that God may change me from the inside out. I hope that Bible study participants, through the study of Scripture, are drawn into an intimate relationship with Jesus Christ.

2. **Fellowship.** Transformation often happens in the midst of community. In that community, one finds encouragement, motivation, accountability, and often loving correction. One of the goals I have with Bible studies is to take individuals from various backgrounds, ages, and personalities and

help create an environment where authentic relationships can be formed for the purpose of spiritual formation and discipleship.

3. **Multiplication.** As people grow spiritually through Bible studies, I hope that it will spur them on to go and make disciples of others and to lead Bible studies of their own. That's how D^2 is supposed to work.

Let's think further about these three goals. In the light of them, my Bible studies have a two-fold purpose.

First, I hope and pray that all participants will gain a better knowledge and understanding of the biblical books or topics being studied so that they may grow spiritually by knowing more about God, his overall plan of redemption, his will, and his purpose for their lives.

Second, I hope and pray that this knowledge and understanding will lead individuals to demonstrate the wisdom they have gained from God's Word by sharing it with those around them at school, at work, and in other places. Having knowledge about a topic of study does not mean an internal change has been made that brings about action.

So, in my Bible studies, I always hope to provide material that will help individuals gain knowledge, then ask questions that will bring understanding, and then motivate participants to go and live the Word of God in the world and to demonstrate godly wisdom. I hope that through these Bible studies, individuals will not only hear, know, and understand the Word, but will also be driven to become the "living word" to the world around them. I constantly ask Bible study teachers and facilitators at my church to go beyond the lessons or curriculum to demonstrate how what they teach can and should be lived daily. We are all the sixty-seventh book of Scripture as we engage the world with the Word of God.

Jean-Pierre de Caussade addresses this idea. "Without knowing it," he says, "all are instruments of that Spirit to bring the message very freshly to the world. And if souls knew how to unite themselves to this purpose, their lives would be a succession of divine Scriptures, continuing till the end of time, not written with ink on paper, but on each human heart. This is what the book of life is about."[7] He believes that the lives of the saints—our lives— are the continuing pages of Scripture and the sequel to the New Testament. The pages of the Bible are therefore the days and events of our lives lived out before others, in the same way that the passages of Scripture have been a recording of the movement of God through the lives of individuals for millennia. The sequel to the New Testament is being written now, by action and suffering. Caussade goes on to say that "the books the Holy Spirit is writing are living, and every soul a volume in which the divine author makes a true revelation of his word, explaining it to every heart, unfolding it in every moment."[8] So are you the living Word of God?

In addition to immersing your heart in God's holy Word, you can find opportunities to connect and grow in your relationship with Christ in the presence of others. You can do this (as a part of your development as a disciple of Christ) by participating in a small group at your church or with one you discover. What is a small group? It's pretty simple. A small group consists of usually no more than fifteen to twenty adults who gather in homes and perhaps share a meal together and have fellowship, prayer, study in God's Word, service projects, outreach opportunities, and mutual support and encouragement in the journey of faith. No matter what form a small group takes, you should find one that provides opportunities for each participant to *grow*.

The purpose of our small groups at my church is to provide growth in individual spiritual maturity, in relationships and connections with the body of Christ, and in bringing others to Christ and into the body of Christ. We want to help all our members and guests experience transformed lives. Whether one is just now becoming interested in God or has walked with him for many years, a small group can be a powerful resource in their quest to be transformed into the image of Christ.

Last, true discipleship is mutual and relational in nature. Why? Because relationships are the conduit of God's love. Therefore, I want to encourage you to focus on becoming more like Christ by building relationships with others, meeting regularly with them, and by holding one another accountable as brothers and sisters in Christ. To accomplish this, I recommend that you form a discipleship group and do the following:

- Identify two or three individuals (for groups of no more than four individuals) who can commit to meet regularly with you during the coming year to grow as a disciple of Christ.
- Have a mentor who works to develop personal relationships with the individuals so that, out of a relationship of love and trust, each one might begin to grow toward spiritual maturity.
- Spend time together going through some sort of discipleship curriculum to foster mutual spiritual growth.
- Work together to develop a personal spiritual growth plan by sharing the level of spiritual maturity you would like to accomplish during your time with this discipleship group.

Experience God by Practicing Spiritual Disciplines

Spiritual disciplines are designed to open up space in our lives for God to meet with us, transform us, and prepare us for his work. Spiritual disciplines are not the same for every person. One may impact one individual and not another. Please remember that they are a means and not the end. Trying new practices regularly will help you to discover new ways to see and connect with God. In the end, the goal is to grow more intimate with God and to hear his voice. I usually practice one spiritual discipline each week to grow closer to God and try new ones from week to week. A lot of resources on spiritual disciplines are out there from which to draw ideas.

Equip Yourself for Ministry by Participating in Your Church

Some types of participation include, but are not be limited to, worship, retreats, seminars, and conferences. Worship is a part of what forms a Christ-centered faith in adults and children (or repels them from it). Worship affects the way we live every day. Therefore, choosing one thing over another is more than a matter of taste and preference in worship. It is a responsibility and an opportunity for discipleship and spiritual formation.

The Latin phrase *lex orandi, lex credendi, lex vivendi* essentially means "how we pray influences what we believe and how we live our lives." By this, we can understand that all aspects of worship influence discipleship and spiritual formation, both for individuals and for groups who have gathered for worship. As I have already noted, spiritual formation can be anything—Christ-centered or not—that forms us from the inside out. Everyone is being formed spiritually, whether for good or evil. What we read, watch, sing, and listen to contributes to the formation of our inner self—our soul and spirit.

The world understands this all too well; advertisers use this concept to shape thought. They don't call it spiritual formation, but they understand that if you change someone's thoughts, you change their actions. Advertisers spend billions of dollars each year to have us believe that their product will somehow make us better. Spiritual formation that happens through television, movies, magazines, and other media is hours longer than the spiritual formation and discipleship that happens through worship each week. While much of this formation happens unconsciously, we must be conscious of and intentional with what we do each worship time and throughout our week (because worship is 24/7, not confined to an hour on a particular day). What we choose to incorporate or participate in as we worship will contribute to or hinder our ability to pray, believe, and ultimately to live each day well as a disciple of Christ.

With that in mind, worship should be fairly simple and designed to keep the focus on God, not ourselves. As you can imagine, every worship assembly isn't going to be exactly the same, but you might participate in some common ingredients each week to help you come before the throne of God; to worship him with all your heart, soul, mind, and strength; and to be formed into the image of Jesus Christ.

Periodically, attend retreats, seminars, and conferences that are designed specifically to help you grow in your faith and relationship with Christ. Some of them may be offered in your local church, and some are at other locations and organized by different groups and organizations. I encourage you to take part in these gatherings regularly for growth, fellowship, and connecting with other disciples who are ever seeking to become more like Christ.

Engage the World through a Committed Response to Jesus

Part of the Great Commission calls us to "go" and "make." We are called as disciples of Christ to go out into the world so that we can be God's light to all people. Jesus shared these words during the Sermon on the Mount: "You are the light of the world. A city set on a hill cannot be hidden. Nor do people light a lamp and put it under a basket, but on a stand, and it gives light to all in the house. In the same way, let your light shine before others, so that they may see your good works and give glory to your Father who is in heaven" (Matt. 5:14–16). God calls us to be his light to the world. By that, I understand him to say that a disciple of Christ is God's servant who actively engages the world by helping others in practical ways. Like Christ, we did not become his disciples to be served, but to serve others. To serve is to sacrifice, and to sacrifice is to give up what may be best for ourselves for the good of others and for the glory of God.

So share in serving God and his people in some way at least once a month as a part of your plan for discipleship. I hope that each person works each day to be a living sacrifice to God, which Paul told the Roman church would be "holy and acceptable to God." He called this kind of service "our spiritual worship" (12:1). I know that finding time to do it each week can be difficult. So start with at least one act of service each month, with hopes that it will grow month after month and week after week.

Acts of service (or the *go* and *make* in the Great Commission) come in many different forms. People only need to open their eyes and see the needs of those around them. God will always present opportunities to engage the world around you through meeting the needs of others, whether those needs are physical or spiritual. Of course, we all recognize that in meeting physical needs, we often meet spiritual needs. We can find many opportunities to serve people both inside and outside of the church. I typically tell people that if you want to connect with others, then go and serve with them.

Part of serving God includes going and being a witness for God. We have the unique privilege of sharing his message of salvation. A disciple intentionally shares his or her faith in Jesus regularly with those who do not know the Lord. It is an honor to share the love and grace of God that has been freely given to us through Christ so that others may know and share in it with us. I encourage everyone to live out this goal of engaging the world through service to God in three specific ways:

1. **Share your faith with others**. The most obvious way to "go and make" is for you to exert a concerted effort to find others you can share your faith with. They can be your neighbors, coworkers, friends, team members, or other people. The point is that you are being deliberate about sharing your faith in Christ with them.

2. **Serve others**. As mentioned just now, serving others by meeting their physical needs is a great opportunity for you to share your faith with them. This can be in the form of giving food to the hungry, providing shelter for the homeless, giving clothes to those without, providing funds for the poor, and many other ways. The options are endless, but those willing to serve are often few. Seek to discover some way each month to serve others instead of yourself.

3. **Become involved in missions**. Missions are another way to serve not only God but also others by meeting their physical, spiritual, and emotional needs. It takes us out of our comfort zone and into a world that God wants us to reach. During those opportunities, you are connecting with God, with those serving with you on the trip, and with those whom you are serving. If you feel like your walk with God has grown stale, then go on a mission trip. Some discover on a mission trip that they want to be in the mission field permanently. For others, they discover that the mission field is wherever they find themselves, and they are now

better equipped to help those around them become disciples of Christ.

Jesus said, "It is more blessed to give than to receive" (Acts 20:35). I believe those words with all my heart. Although some people are truly gifted by the Holy Spirit in this area, I firmly believe that the Bible teaches us that all disciples are to engage the world through good works and sharing their faith. Make this a part of your plan: be a true disciple of Jesus Christ who makes disciples.

The Plan in Action

There you have it. A blueprint for discipleship. D^2 in action! In the preceding pages, I hope that I have outlined for you what I believe God is asking of us as his disciples. As you may have noted, much of what I said so far in this chapter has focused more on what you can do as an individual. But I want to encourage you to live this out with others in your local church, because our lives as disciples are meant to be shared in community rather than isolation.

It is important to note here that to really get involved in D^2— to truly carry out this purpose and mission of discipleship—you will have to be "all in." All in means you must be practicing these words, not just reading them. Going all in means recognizing that you must not do some things you currently are doing in order to allow time for intentional discipleship. I firmly believe this is God's call, his mission, and his purpose for us both individually and as the family of God. Therefore, I challenge you to work toward this mission every day.

I recognize that we will all have times when we will fall short of this goal. We will make mistakes and sometimes take wrong paths. But we must commit that we will not allow shortcomings to halt God's progress in us, as weak as we are. God's power is made perfect through our weakness. When we are weak, *he* makes us strong (2 Cor. 12:1–10). So let us move forward with this mission in mind. Let us do so unapologetically and with great zeal, no longer making excuses for why we have not carried out God's Greatest Things (loving God, loving others, and going and making disciples). Instead, let us be full of resolve to make every effort to become the disciples Jesus has called us to be.

I hope you will work through the following pages and pray over them as you make a plan for the coming year. You should do this with others so that you have accountability throughout the year. The intention here is that you will not be reactive in your spiritual growth (engaging things as they come), but proactive (planning for growth). I ask that you join me in these efforts as a part of God's family so that we (both individually and collectively) can bring glory and honor to God and can allow his light to shine through us in this dark world. May all we do be pleasing to him, our God and our king. Through God we *go*!

Plan for Spiritual Growth

Use the following pages to create your plan for spiritual growth. Remember, this process goes on throughout your life. Therefore, you should do this each year so that you can continue in your growth rather than becoming complacent and apathetic. There are no right or wrong answers here. This is your plan. You are not required to do everything each quarter, but do make a strategy as to what you want to do.

Use the help of your accountability partners or discipleship group to help you discover your areas of growth and to hold you to your commitment. Before you begin, spend time in prayer and fasting. Ask God to help you discover the ways in which you can grow closer to him and help others do so as well. Trust that he will answer you in the affirmative. May God bless you!

D²

Name: _____

Accountability or Discipleship Partner(s): _____

_____

Beginning Date: _____

Current Phase of Spiritual Growth (circle one):

Spiritual Infancy   Spiritual Childhood   Spiritual Adolescence
Spiritual Adulthood   Spiritual Maturity

Plan for Spiritual Growth Covenant
I believe that my relationship with God is the most important relationship in my life. Therefore, I give priority to him in all things. This *Plan for Spiritual Growth* is my covenant between God, my accountability or discipleship partner(s), and me. I ask you, Father, to draw us closer together through these efforts as I open myself up to your Spirit's transformative work in my life. My desire is that your Spirit will transform me into the image of your Son, my Savior, Jesus Christ. May your will be done in my life.

_____
(My Signature)

_____
(Partner Signature)

_____
(Partner Signature)

First Quarter (the months of _____ to _____)

During this first quarter, I will do the following:

Love God by . . .

Studying and meditating on God's word by

_____

_____

_____

Praying daily by

_____

_____

_____

Practicing spiritual disciplines by

_____

_____

_____

Being a part of a Bible study or prayer group by

_____

_____

_____

Doing the following things to connect with God:

_____

_____

_____

Love others by . . .

Getting a spiritual guide or mentor

_____

(name of guide or mentor)

Attending church services and gatherings regularly

Being part of a growth group, including (list names)

_____

_____

_____

Serving others by

_____

_____

_____

Becoming involved in a ministry group (list group or groups)

_____

_____

_____

Becoming involved in missions by

_____

_____

_____

Doing the following things to connect with others:

_____

_____

_____

Go and make disciples by . . .

Sharing my faith with others by

_____

_____

_____

Serving others by

_____

_____

_____

Becoming involved in missions by

_____

_____

_____

Doing the following things to "go and make disciples":

_____

_____

_____

To grow more and more into the image of Christ, I need to repent of and allow the Holy Spirit to change and transform the following areas in my life:

_____

_____

_____

_____

_____

_____

_____

_____

_____

_____

_____

_____

_____

_____

_____

_____

_____

Second Quarter (the months of _____ to _____)

During the second quarter, I will do the following:

Love God by . . .

Studying and meditating on God's word by

_____

_____

_____

Praying daily by

_____

_____

_____

Practicing spiritual disciplines by

_____

_____

_____

Being a part of a Bible study or prayer group by

_____

_____

_____

Doing the following things to connect with God:

_____

_____

_____

Love others by . . .

Getting a spiritual guide or mentor

_____

(name of guide or mentor)

Attending church services and gatherings regularly

Being part of a growth group, including (list names)

_____

_____

_____

Serving others by

_____

_____

_____

Becoming involved in a ministry group (list group or groups)

_____

_____

_____

Becoming involved in missions by

_____

_____

_____

Doing the following things to connect with others:

_____

_____

_____

Go and make disciples by . . .

Sharing my faith with others by

_____

_____

_____

Serving others by

_____

_____

_____

Becoming involved in missions by

_____

_____

_____

Doing the following things to "go and make disciples":

_____

_____

_____

To grow more and more into the image of Christ, I need to repent of and allow the Holy Spirit to change and transform the following areas in my life:

_____

_____

_____

_____

_____

_____

_____

_____

_____

_____

_____

_____

_____

_____

_____

_____

_____

Third Quarter (the months of _____ to _____)

During the third quarter, I will do the following:

Love God by . . .

Studying and meditating on God's word by

_____

_____

_____

Praying daily by

_____

_____

_____

Practicing spiritual disciplines by

_____

_____

_____

Being a part of a Bible study or prayer group by

_____

_____

_____

Doing the following things to connect with God:

_____

_____

_____

Love others by . . .

Getting a spiritual guide or mentor

_____

(name of guide or mentor)

Attending church services and gatherings regularly

Being part of a growth group, including (list names)

_____
_____
_____

Serving others by

_____
_____
_____

Becoming involved in a ministry group (list group or groups)

_____
_____
_____

Becoming involved in missions by

_____
_____
_____

Doing the following things to connect with others:

_____
_____
_____

Go and make disciples by . . .
Sharing my faith with others by

_____
_____
_____

Serving others by

_____
_____
_____

Becoming involved in missions by

_____
_____
_____

Doing the following things to "go and make disciples":

_____
_____
_____

To grow more and more into the image of Christ, I need to repent of and allow the Holy Spirit to change and transform the following areas in my life:

_____
_____
_____
_____
_____
_____
_____
_____
_____
_____
_____
_____
_____
_____
_____
_____
_____
_____
_____
_____

Fourth Quarter (the months of _____ to _____)

During this quarter, I will do the following:

Love God by . . .

Studying and meditating on God's word by

_____

_____

_____

Praying daily by

_____

_____

_____

Practicing spiritual disciplines by

_____

_____

_____

Being a part of a Bible study or prayer group by

_____

_____

_____

Doing the following things to connect with God:

_____

_____

_____

Love others by . . .

Getting a spiritual guide or mentor

_____

(name of guide or mentor)

Attending church services and gatherings regularly

Being part of a growth group, including (list names)

_____

_____

_____

Serving others by

_____

_____

_____

Becoming involved in a ministry group (list group or groups)

_____

_____

_____

Becoming involved in missions by

_____

_____

_____

Doing the following things to connect with others:

_____

_____

_____

Go and make disciples by . . .

Sharing my faith with others by

_____

_____

_____

Serving others by

_____

_____

_____

D²

Becoming involved in missions by

_____

_____

_____

Doing the following things to "go and make disciples":

_____

_____

_____

To grow more and more into the image of Christ, I need to repent of and allow the Holy Spirit to change and transform the following areas in my life:

_____

_____

_____

_____

_____

_____

_____

_____

_____

_____

_____

_____

_____

_____

_____

_____

_____

_____

_____

_____

Post-Plan Evaluation

Current Phase of Spiritual Growth after this year (circle one):

Spiritual Infancy   Spiritual Childhood   Spiritual Adolescence
Spiritual Adulthood   Spiritual Maturity

What have I learned about myself and my growth as a disciple of Christ?

_____

_____

_____

_____

_____

_____

What have I learned about God and my relationship with him?

_____

_____

_____

_____

_____

_____

What are my next steps toward spiritual growth?

_____

_____

_____

_____

_____

_____

Notes

Chapter 1: Follow Me

[1] C. S. Lewis, *Mere Christianity* (New York: HarperCollins, 1980), 177, 199 (emphasis added). Kindle.

[2] Or what some have termed the "Four B's": butts, buildings, baptisms, and budgets. Mike McDaniel, *The Resurgent Church: 7 Critical Ways to Thrive in the New Post-Christendom World* (Nashville: Thomas Nelson, 2016), 99.

[3] Dallas Willard, *The Divine Conspiracy: Rediscovering Our Hidden Life in God* (San Francisco: HarperCollins, 1998), 300–1.

[4] I accessed the following information from their website (http://www .ccfairfax.org/) as of 2016.

[5] Dietrich Bonhoeffer, *Discipleship* (Minneapolis, MN: Fortress Press, 2001), 43.

[6] Bonhoeffer, *Discipleship*, 43.

[7] Bonhoeffer, *Discipleship*, 44.

[8] Quoted from Brennan Manning's *The Signature of Jesus*; and Catherine Martin's *Pilgrimage of the Heart*.

Chapter 2: Two Truths—D²

[1] Wayne Grudem, *Systematic Theology: An Introduction to Biblical Doctrine* (Grand Rapids: Zondervan, 1994), 443–44 [see footnotes]; Anthony H. Hoekema, *Created in God's Image* (Grand Rapids: Eerdmans, 1986), 13–15, 35.

[2] Kenneth A. Mathews, "Genesis 1–11:26," *The New American Commentary*, vol. 1A (Nashville: Broadman and Holman, 1996), 167–68.

Chapter 3: Untangling Discipleship

[1] Michael J. Wilkins, *Following the Master: Discipleship in the Steps of Jesus* (Grand Rapids: Zondervan, 1992), 40.

[2] Eric Geiger, Michael Kelley, and Philip Nation, *Transformational Discipleship: How People Really Grow* (Nashville: B&H Publishing Group, 2012), 16.

[3] Jim Putman, Bobby Harrington William, and Robert Coleman, *DiscipleShift: Five Steps That Help Your Church to Make Disciples Who Make Disciples, Exponential Series* (Grand Rapids: Zondervan, 2013), 31.

[4] Putman, William, and Coleman, *DiscipleShift*, 46–51.

[5] Dallas Willard, *The Divine Conspiracy: Rediscovering Our Hidden Life in God* (San Francisco: HarperCollins, 1998), 281.

[6] Willard, *The Divine Conspiracy*, 282.

[7] Willard, *The Divine Conspiracy*, 283.

[8] Willard, *The Divine Conspiracy*, 283–84.

[9] Bill Hull, *The Complete Book of Discipleship: On Being and Making Followers of Christ* (Colorado Springs: NavPress, 2006), 24–25.

[10] Hull, *The Complete Book of Discipleship*, 25.

[11] Wilkins, *Following the Master*, 41.

[12] Hull, *The Complete Book of Discipleship*, 24.

[13] Wilkins, *Following the Master*, 41.

[14] Wilkins, *Following the Master*, 41.

Chapter 4: Holy and Wholly Living

[1] Christopher J. H. Wright, *Deuteronomy*, Understanding the Bible Commentary Series (Grand Rapids: Baker Books, 1994), 99.

[2] Duane L. Christensen, *Deuteronomy*, Word Biblical Commentary (Grand Rapids: Zondervan, 1991), 143.

[3] Eugene Merrill, *Deuteronomy*, The New American Commentary, vol. 4 (Nashville: B&H Publishing Group, 1994), 164.

[4] Christensen, *Deuteronomy*, 143.

Chapter 5: What Does a Disciple Look Like?

[1] Kenneth Boa, *Conformed to His Image: Biblical and Practical Approaches to Spiritual Formation* (Grand Rapids: Zondervan, 2001), 294.

[2] Boa, *Conformed to His Image*, 294.

[3] A. W. Tozer, *Paths to Power: Living in the Spirit's Fullness* (Camp Hill, PA: WingSpread, 1964), 39.

Chapter 6: Developing a Plan for Spiritual Growth

[1]Greg Ogden, *The Essential Commandment: A Disciple's Guide to Loving God and Others* (Downers Grove, IL: InterVarsity Press Connect, 2011), 153.

[2]Ogden, *The Essential Commandment*, 153.

[3]James A. Brooks, *Mark*, The New American Commentary, vol. 23 (Nashville: Broadman & Holman Publishers, 1991), 198.

[4]William L. Lane, *The Gospel of Mark*, New International Commentary on the New Testament (Grand Rapids: Eerdmans, 1974), 433.

[5]D. A. Carson, *The Gospel according to John*, The Pillar New Testament Commentary (Leicester, England: APOLLOS, 1991), 484. British spellings retained.

Chapter 7: Discipleship Blueprint

[1]Henri J. M. Nouwen, *With Open Hands* (Notre Dame, IN: Ave Maria Press, 1992), 19.

[2]Brennan Manning, *The Ragamuffin Gospel: Good News for the Bedraggled, Beat-Up, and Burnt Out* (Sisters, OR: Multnomah Books, 2005), 155–56.

[3]Manning, *The Ragamuffin Gospel*, 156.

[4] Albert George Lemmons, *Teach Us to Pray*, rev. ed. (Nashville: Pollock Printing, 2000), 1.

[5]Lemmons, *Teach Us to Pray*, 4.

[6]Dallas Willard, "Spiritual Formation in Christ for the Whole Life and Whole Person," *VOCATIO* 12, no. 2 (Spring 2001): 7.

[7]Jean Pierre de Caussade, *The Sacrament of the Present Moment* (San Francisco: Harper & Row, 1982), 73–74.

[8]Caussade, *The Sacrament of the Present Moment*, 73–74.